WORLD CUP 1998: SCOTLAND'S STORY

THE FRANCE 98 JOURNEY

NEIL DOHERTY

Copyright © 2021 by Neil Doherty

All rights reserved.

No part of this book may be reproduced in any form or by any electronic or mechanical means, including information storage and retrieval systems, without written permission from the author, except for the use of brief quotations in a book review.

ISBN: 9798745926341

Edited by Alex Hazle.

Cover design by James Pople.

Cover image by Action Images / Stuart Franklin.

Cover image rights licence from Alamy.

For Dad

CONTENTS

1. The Largs Mafia	1
2. Craig Who?	13
3. Brown's Inverted Pyramid	33
4. The Squad	57
5. Smell the Glove	75
6. Blattered	88
7. Sizing Up the Opposition	96
8. A Spaceship On Tap Ae It	126
9. Brazil	138
10. Norway	165
11. Morocco	193
12. After the Carnival	211
Afterword	231
About the Author	237
Acknowledgements	239
References & Bibliography	241

1
THE LARGS MAFIA

The 20th-century history of the Scotland National Team at the FIFA World Cup finals is a dramatic story spanning eight tournaments, beginning in 1954 and concluding in 1998. It is a story that features, or at least cameos, most of Scotland's football greats, such as Jock Stein, Kenny Dalglish, Denis Law and Alex Ferguson. It is a story that captivated the Scottish public over six World Cup tournaments between 1974 and 1998, during which the Tartan Army and Scottish media travelled all over the globe hoping to witness football glory. It is a typically Scottish story, blending vain hope with sharp realism and unimaginable bad luck, with flashes of joy that made the journey worthwhile. Other writers have covered this ground brilliantly, most notably Archie Macpherson in his 2018 book, *Adventures in the Golden Age*, which beautifully chronicles his time as a commentator and journalist over six tournaments. In contrast, I tell just one story, Scotland at France 98, which in some ways encapsulates everything that had gone before, and explains much that has come since, regarding Scotland's relationship with the World Cup.

My fascination with the Scotland National Team, and the corresponding content for this book, has its origins in the first international match I attended, Scotland versus Bulgaria at Hampden Park on 10 September 1986. Ironically, the aforementioned Archie Macpherson, who has witnessed as many Scotland internationals as anyone, summed up this match as 'probably the worst international game I have ever seen'. As a youngster I was not put off, as I was already steeped in football by my father, a fellow football obsessive who had followed Scotland to the World Cup in West Germany in 1974. I have since learned that the 35,000 attendance at the old Hampden Park that night was considered low, but as a small boy who had been initiated into live football by watching Kilmarnock play in the second tier of Scottish football, I was mesmerised. In terms of historical importance, this was Scotland's first competitive match since the World Cup in Mexico in 1986, and was the first match in charge for the recent surprise managerial appointment, 43-year-old Scottish Football Association (SFA) Director of Coaching, Andy Roxburgh. This appointment was the decision of the late Ernie Walker, SFA Secretary at the time, who had witnessed first-hand the catastrophe of previous Scottish World Cup efforts and had sought to set the Scotland National Team on an altogether different trajectory.

Roxburgh's tenure was initially overshadowed by the infamous tabloid headline, 'Andy Who?' – a sentiment shared by large sections of the Scottish public and media at the time. Roxburgh was replacing Alex Ferguson, no less, who had been a temporary replacement for the late Jock Stein. Stein, who had presided over Celtic's greatest era, had tragically and dramatically died from a pulmonary oedema at Ninian Park, Cardiff, following Scotland's 1–1 draw with

Wales in the final qualification match for the 1986 World Cup in September 1985. Even a small boy like me knew enough about the game to ask why Roxburgh was appointed ahead of a hero known to me through my fascination with Panini stickers and football history books. Today I am grateful for Walker's progressive decision in July 1986, and my father's corresponding decision to take me to the 'worst ever' international game, as it has provided such meaningful context for my first book.

In order to look ahead, however, it is useful to look back briefly. In his seminal book, *Inverting the Pyramid: The History of Football Tactics*, Jonathan Wilson reminds us that the nation of Scotland played an integral role in the invention of the sport of football. Following the first written rules emerging from England's public schools in the 1840s, and the English rule development in 1863 to outlaw carrying the ball by hand, Scotland competed with England in the first ever international match in 1872. The SFA was then formed in 1873, with the game in Scotland having previously been governed by Scotland's oldest football club, Queen's Park, which was formed in 1867.

In the immediate years that followed, Scottish and English clubs, in the context of their cross-border rivalry with each other, between them developed the first recognised formation – a 2-3-5 formation, 'the pyramid' – and two opposing football styles. Scotland favoured what was referred to as 'the passing game', with England favouring 'the dribbling game'. These early tactical ideas were then exported around the globe by pioneering coaches such as Englishman Jimmy Hogan, who coached his favoured

Scottish passing game in Hungary and the Netherlands. Football thereafter spread like wildfire throughout Europe, and South America followed suit, with enormous British investment in Argentina, Brazil, Uruguay, Colombia and Chile leading to tens of thousands of Britons emigrating to these countries at the end of the 19th century. The British founded countless football clubs across the South American continent, where the impoverished nationals watched the British play football from the sidelines or from rooftops, before creating their own working-class equivalent on urban back streets and wasteland. Consistently, the 2–3–5 formation was accepted and integrated from nation to nation, and was largely viewed as the only way to set up a football team. Using the terminology of the era, the 2–3–5 comprised two full-backs, three half-backs and five forwards.

Despite having played a lead role in the creation and global export of football, Scotland do not feature too strongly in the initial tactical developments of the early 20th century. Nations such as Hungary, Austria, Italy, Germany and the Soviet Union supplanted Scotland in Europe when it came to the progression of football tactics. Likewise, Uruguay, Brazil and Argentina quickly advanced and moved ahead of Scotland in the area of tactical development. English football also evolved, with early Arsenal manager Herbert Chapman credited with the first formation that deviated from the 2–3–5. In 1925, the new offside rule reduced the requirement from three players to two between a forward and the opposition goal for a forward to be onside, a rule that had remained unchanged since 1866. This led to an immediate increase in goals, and Arsenal's Chapman took the radical step of fielding three defenders, in what became known as the W–M formation, due to the attacking and defending players forming the shapes of these letters on formational team sheets.

The inaugural FIFA World Cup was held in Uruguay in 1930 – however, it would be another 24 years before Scotland would first play at the finals. Scotland's participation at the World Cup could have begun in Brazil in 1950, a tournament to which the SFA received an invitation but which they farcically declined on the basis that Scotland did not belong in the tournament if they could not win the British Championship. England then won the British Championship, and Scotland endured the SFA's self-imposed exile from Brazil 1950!

Scotland's first two attempts at World Cup glory therefore began at the tournaments held in Switzerland in 1954 and Sweden in 1958. Scotland's participation at these tournaments is now a historical footnote, and was characterised by SFA bungling. For example, following Scotland's first ever World Cup match on 16 June 1954, a respectable 1–0 defeat by Austria, a nation steeped in football history, the SFA travelling delegation intervened, stating that they would pick the team for the next match. Manager Andy Beattie quit immediately, leaving Scotland without a manager to face holders Uruguay. Scotland were subsequently thrashed 7–0 by Uruguay in Basel on 19 June, with the Scottish players almost fainting in the heat due to wearing thick woollen kits provided by the SFA, who had assumed Switzerland was covered in snow and ice even in the summer!

1958 in Sweden was no better, with Scotland unbelievably entering the tournament with no manager. The Munich air disaster in February 1958 had ruled out iconic Manchester United manager Matt Busby, who had been lined up to take charge for the World Cup. The SFA opted not to appoint a replacement and picked the squad for the tournament via their own selection committee, which was a standard practice of the era. Goalkeeper Tommy Younger was left to take the team talks, and the squad squabbled with the SFA over unpaid expenses before limping out of the tournament with one point from three matches.

Within contemporary football history, Scotland's national team or clubs do not feature too much again until 1967, when Celtic, under Jock Stein, became the first British club to lift the European Cup. In the final, held at Portugal's Estádio Nacional just outside capital Lisbon, Celtic's 'Lisbon Lions', as they were soon nicknamed, faced the mighty Inter Milan, who had become famous for the notorious defensive style known as *catenaccio* (meaning 'the chain'). The leading exponent of *catenaccio* was the charismatic Inter manager of the era, Helenio Herrera. Herrera was an Argentinian, born to Spanish parents, who had spent his playing career in France before progressing to club management in the late 1940s. Herrera could possibly be considered the first modern football manager or head coach, with methods which incorporated psychology, diet and lifestyle. He demanded absolute discipline, fitness and professionalism. Between 1962 and 1966, Herrera's Inter swept all before them, winning Serie A three times and the European Cup twice. However, the *catenaccio* style was synonymous with gamesmanship, and the dirty tactics applied by Inter won them few admirers on the continent. Tactically, Herrera's Inter were ultra-defensive, having led the evolution of the W–M formation to include a sweeper behind the defensive line, known as a *libero*, thus creating the first formation that fielded four defenders.

Another of Scotland's first footballing household names, Liverpool manager Bill Shankly, hated Herrera's style. This was in no small part due to Liverpool's exit from the 1965 European Cup at the hands of Inter, following a tie characterised by *catenaccio* gamesmanship. However, in the lead-up to the 1967 final, Stein did not allow Herrera's famous mind games to unnerve him. This was despite Herrera arriving in Glasgow on a private jet to watch Celtic face Rangers in the Old Firm derby. During this episode, Herrera also initially invited Stein to join him for the return journey to Italy to watch Inter face Juventus, before withdrawing the invitation and insulting Stein, stating that his plane would not fit a man of his girth. Stein had wisely declined the invitation, correctly calculating Herrera was playing mind games. Stein did travel to Turin of his own accord, to find the taxi and match tickets also promised by Herrera had not been provided.

The mind games Stein played with Herrera in revenge are now the stuff of football folklore, and were passed to pupils such as Alex Ferguson, who later also steered a Scottish club to European success, using only Scottish players, when his Aberdeen side won the Cup Winners' Cup in 1983 – one such mind game was to gift their opposite manager a bottle of whisky on the eve of a big European match to create the illusion of being a servile smaller club. The 1967 final itself was poetic revenge for Stein, with Celtic's 2–1 victory in an ultra-attacking 4–2–4 formation widely considered a victory for the sport of football. Celtic's win also spelled the end of *catenaccio*, as Inter's players thereafter could no longer tolerate Herrera's ends-justify-the-means football. This was, fittingly, also the last noteworthy stand of football's original ultra-attacking formations, which had originated in football's infancy on the playing fields of Scotland and England.

Scotland did not qualify for the World Cup finals again

until West Germany 1974, and thereafter qualified for five consecutive tournaments between 1974 and 1990. Scotland then failed to qualify for the World Cup in the USA in 1994, but rediscovered the qualification formula for France 98. This golden era created a perception within Scottish society that the Tartan Army belonged at the World Cup every four years, and how Scotland fared in the group stages of the tournament was the yardstick used to measure success. Readers born after 1998, starved of Scottish involvement in a major tournament for 23 years prior to Euro 2020, may find it difficult to comprehend the sense of entitlement that once existed in Scotland in relation to World Cup qualification. Although Scotland have never qualified for the second round of the World Cup finals, the accomplishments of their top players from this bygone era eclipse the records of more recent Scottish internationals. Take Joe Jordan, who scored at three separate tournaments, in 1974, 1978 and 1982. Kenny Dalglish played eight matches and scored two goals across the same three tournaments. Goalkeeper Jim Leighton was included in all four World Cup squads between 1982 and 1998, and accumulated a Scottish-record nine World Cup appearances across three tournaments. We will come to Leighton later, as his France 98 story is one of the many fascinating subplots that emerged as the competition for squad places reached fever pitch in the lead-up to France 98.

The draw for France 98, a grandiose five-day function held in the Stade Vélodrome, Marseille, in December 1997, was responsible for this fever pitch. In Marseille, the footballing gods (perhaps with some assistance from FIFA delegates who acted like gods) decreed Scotland would face Brazil in the opening match of France 98 on 10 June 1998, creating the biggest fixture in the history of the Scotland

National Team. Some may argue that other Scotland matches should be ranked higher in terms of importance, but the opening match of the World Cup is second only to the World Cup Final itself as a global football spectacle in a showpiece event occurring only once every four years. In 1998, the World Cup was expected to attract a cumulative TV viewership of 40 billion, more than six times the world's population at the time.

So, exactly how did the Scotland National Team of 1998 find itself competing in this privileged fixture, and who was the architect of Scotland's France 98 qualification? Despite being a lifelong football fanatic, I must concede that I knew only a basic outline of the career of former Scotland manager Craig Brown prior to writing this book. In 1998, I was an ordinary punter who did not have spare money to travel to France, and I watched the World Cup while drinking lager in my favourite pub. On this basis, I have assumed that others interested in reading this book might also be similarly unaware of Craig Brown's credentials. The story of Scotland at France 98 cannot be properly understood without gaining an understanding of Brown's background, personality and football methodology. This in itself is an intriguing story of a learning culture with a global reputation, fostered in the unlikely setting of Largs, North Ayrshire, which in essence is where Scotland's France 98 story begins.

In 1975, eight years after Jock Stein's incredible European success had put Scotland back on the football map, Andy Roxburgh was appointed as the SFA's first Director of Coaching at Inverclyde National Sports Training Centre,

Largs. The centre is known in football circles simply as 'Inverclyde' – confusingly, seeing as it sits in North Ayrshire and not neighbouring Inverclyde at all. It is named after Lord Inverclyde, former president of the Scottish Council for Physical Recreation, who was responsible for establishing the centre in 1956. The building itself was built in the 19th century as an extravagant residence, before falling into disrepair as a hotel in the 1920s, and finding new life as Scotland's home of sport from the 1960s onwards. Roxburgh, a former player with Queen's Park, East Stirlingshire, Partick Thistle, Falkirk and Clydebank, was just 32 years old when appointed. Impressively, Roxburgh, a physical education graduate, had also previously been the youngest school headmaster in Scotland, and had qualified as an SFA coach in 1966 at the age of 24.

Similarly, Craig Brown had obtained his SFA preliminary badge and A Licence at Inverclyde in the mid-1960s, and likewise obtained a degree in physical education and pursued a career in teaching. Prior to Roxburgh's 1975 appointment, Brown had been invited to join the Inverclyde coaching team by Roy Small, who was in charge of the SFA courses at the time. In his autobiography, *The Game of My Life*, Brown recollects that the Inverclyde staff at the time comprised Scottish managers of the era such as Eddie Turnbull (Aberdeen), Jimmy Bonthrone (East Fife), Wilson Humphries (St Mirren), Archie Robertson (Clyde) and Willie Ormond (St Johnstone), as well as former Hibernian player Peter Rice.

Interestingly, progressive thinker Brown was not initially invited back to Inverclyde, after a fallout with Rice over the tactics used by former Hearts and Aberdeen player Eddie Thomson, who was taking a course under Brown's mentorship. Brown remembers Thomson used five defenders in a sweeper system in one of his modules, and Rice instructed Brown to fail Thomson for using an unrealistic tactical system. Brown had been impressed with the session and refused to fail Thomson on this basis, while discouraging Rice from thinking about football tactics so rigidly. Rice's displeasure was perhaps a legacy of Scottish hatred of the *catenaccio* system used by Inter and denounced as anti-football by Shankly and Stein. Brown, on the other hand, considered the principle of tactical flexibility to be of the highest importance, and dissuaded young coaches from becoming too attached to one system or set formula.

Another issue facing ambitious young coaches like Roxburgh and Brown was the Scottish cultural distrust of intellect, which framed learning as something to be viewed with suspicion and avoided. In *Inverting the Pyramid*, Jonathan Wilson affirms that this prejudice has plagued British football in general since the earliest days of the sport, and is the reason why so many other nations very quickly overtook British football tactically. Roxburgh, Brown and other coaches sought to break this mould.

However, a faction within Scottish football still tried to reject this new culture of learning, leading to Brown and Roxburgh receiving the tabloid nickname of 'the Largs Mafia'. Today, thankfully, football has moved on, with young players and coaches steeped in the reality that football is a profession and obtaining qualifications is the way to progress. This interesting dynamic now sees millionaire players sharing classroom space with relatively unknown coaches in pursuit of the coveted UEFA Pro Licence. In *The Game of My Life*, Brown credits Frank Coulston, Ross Mathie, Jim Sinclair and Jim Fleeting as the backbone of the successful Largs Football Development Department, and apologises for his own intermittent presence at Largs as his coaching career progressed.

Although the SFA have since moved their courses to the Toryglen Indoor Football Centre, by Hampden Park in Glasgow, and the £33-million purpose-built Oriam, in Edinburgh, Inverclyde has its own place in the annals of Scottish and European football history. Indeed, BBC Sport noted that at the start of the 2011–12 season, nine of the English Premier League's managers had trained or taught at Inverclyde: Alex Ferguson (Manchester United), Kenny Dalglish (Liverpool), David Moyes (Everton), André Villas-Boas (Chelsea), Brendan Rodgers (Swansea City), Roy Hodgson (West Bromwich Albion), Owen Coyle (Bolton Wanderers), Alex McLeish (Aston Villa) and Steve Kean (Blackburn Rovers).

In Europe, Portugal in particular hold Scotland's coaching courses in high esteem, with José Mourinho famously taking his coaching badges at Inverclyde in 2000 while still at Barcelona working under Louis van Gaal. Villas-Boas likewise remains a strong advocate for Scottish coaching, and when speaking at the SFA Pro Licence course in 2018, he said: 'I have lost count how many people I have recommended to [sic] come to Scotland. My nephew, who is 17, is now in Scotland doing his B Licence, too. So, all of this is [due to] the love I have for the courses here [in Scotland]. The quality is the story. It is now Nuno [Espirito Santo], José [Mourinho] and myself. So many have been, though, from our Portuguese [methodology], which is extremely good. But we come to Scotland to get these courses because their level is quite high. And the content that we find here in Scotland, and the friendly environment, [make] you want to come back to keep on with the learning process. It is very good.'

2

CRAIG WHO?

Craig Brown was born on 1 July 1940, and his earliest memories are from tenement life in Corkerhill, Glasgow during the Second World War. As a very young child, Brown recalls the air raids, and being sheltered by his mother as German bombs rained down on Glasgow. Brown's father, Hugh, was in the RAF and was a professional footballer, playing for King's Park (now Stirling Albion) and Hamilton Academical. In *The Game of My Life*, Brown recollects his father also playing for Wolverhampton Wanderers when stationed with the RAF in England, and striking up a firm friendship with Wolves' manager of the era, Ted Vizard, who would later visit Brown's home when visiting Scotland. After the war, Brown's father became a prominent PE teacher, and the family – which also included Brown's two younger brothers, Jock and Bob – settled in Hamilton, where Brown attended Hamilton Academy.

Growing up, Craig Brown identified himself as a supporter of Hamilton Academical and Queens Park, and his favourite footballer was Dave Mackay, then of Hearts but who later won the English double with Spurs in 1961. Brown was an exceptional youth footballer and was a Scotland Under-18 international alongside Billy McNeill, who later would famously captain Celtic's Lisbon Lions in 1967. Brown recalls being aware of the interest in his signature from professional clubs as a schoolboy but being shielded from such matters by his father, who spoke to the clubs on his behalf. Brown also excelled at golf, taking part in competitions and holding a 4 handicap while a schoolboy. Brown also remembers facing Alex Ferguson as a youth footballer and initially training at Celtic with Billy McNeill, before signing for Rangers at age 17.

Rangers manager Scot Symon immediately sent newly-signed Brown out on loan to junior club Coltness United. Brown excelled in his season in junior football and was capped as a Scottish Junior international. Brown's schedule was gruelling at the time as he continued his education and worked as a steelworks labourer. After his successful season on loan, Brown was called up to Ibrox as a full-timer and graduated to play for Rangers reserves alongside stars of the era such as Eric Caldow, Ralph Brand and Johnny Hubbard. Parallel to his football career, Brown also secured himself a place on a three-year course at Jordanhill College to train as a PE teacher. Typically, Brown's day would start with swimming at Cranstonhill Baths, followed by a full day of training at his PE course. Later in the day, he would travel to Ibrox for training with Rangers, which took place in the evening in those days and comprised hard running under fitness trainer Dave Kinnear, later described by Brown as a strict, military-type gentleman. Brown was contending for the left-half position in the Rangers first team. After 18 months at Ibrox without a first-team appearance, Brown recalls Rangers signing another left midfielder, future club legend Jim Baxter. Baxter made an immediate impact, while the unfortunate Brown suffered a serious knee injury that kept him on the periphery at Rangers.

In late 1960, Dundee manager Bob Shankly, brother of iconic Liverpool manager Bill, attempted to sign Brown. Rangers initially turned down Dundee, but after negotiations they agreed to let Brown leave on loan. Brown describes being keen on this move at the time, as he feared his playing career was sinking into stagnation at Ibrox. Unfortunately, after just a few matches in Dundee's reserves, Brown's left knee began troubling him again. This led to surgery, but in the days before keyhole surgery this meant many months on the sidelines for the unfortunate Brown.

After this injury-disrupted loan spell, Brown prepared to return to Ibrox for the 1961–62 season. To his surprise, Bob Shankly then made another bid to sign him, and this time Rangers accepted. Brown recalls mixed feelings on leaving the Scottish champions for Dundee, but feeling hopeful the transfer would kickstart his playing career. Unbelievably, Dundee won the Scottish League Championship for the only time in their history in that first season. In an era before substitutes were permitted, Brown was one of only 15 first-team players Dundee used in their greatest-ever season. In what became typical of Brown's playing career, having won a first-team spot he missed the run-in and watched the final-day celebrations from hospital after his left knee broke down in an away match versus Raith Rovers. In the final highlight of his playing career, Brown was also part of the Dundee squad that reached the European Cup semi-final the following season, an experience Brown later reflected was crucially important as he entered football management. Despite his talent, Brown made only 14 first-team appearances for Dundee before transferring to Falkirk, where he made only 17 more before retiring through injury in 1967 after 31 senior appearances. Nonetheless, Brown retired with a Scottish League Championship winner's medal, a considerable achievement for any Scottish footballer, especially one with so few senior appearances!

After 1967, Brown began working as a primary teacher and a PE teacher. By this time, he had also obtained his SFA coaching certificate, his preliminary badge and his A Licence badge at Inverclyde. As outlined in the preceding chapter, by 1969 Brown had been invited to join the coaching team at Inverclyde and was also heavily involved in schools and youth team coaching. Ever the academic, Brown also completed a BA degree with the Open University with the aim of progressing in the teaching profession. This led to Brown securing a deputy headteacher post, and then one as headteacher, before settling as a lecturer at Craigie College of Education in Ayr. Brown and his family then relocated from Hamilton to Prestwick, South Ayrshire.

In the 1975–76 season, Brown accepted an offer from Motherwell to become part-time assistant manager to Willie McLean, elder brother of renowned Scottish football brothers Jim and Tommy McLean. In *The Game of My Life*, Brown concedes that, prior to this offer, he had been somewhat frustrated at no longer being involved at the highest level of Scottish football, as he felt he had more to offer following a playing career cut short by injury. This led to him holding two full-time jobs, as he remained committed to his career in education. Brown additionally concedes that his home life suffered as a result of leaving early each morning and not returning home until late.

At Motherwell, Brown learned from McLean, whom he later described as a master of coaching, tactical awareness and man management, and whom he states taught him more than any other manager during his career. High praise indeed, but typical of Brown's perfectionism and eye for detail, he also saw room for improvement in McLean's relationships with Motherwell's non-playing staff. The 1975–76 season in Scotland was the last of the old two-division system, and a top-ten finish in the old First Division would guarantee a spot in the newly created Scottish Premier Division. Motherwell finished tenth under McLean and Brown, and claimed their spot in the new-look Scottish top flight.

Brown describes his ambitions towards management growing during his time at Motherwell, and in July 1977 he took over as manager of Clyde, following a recommendation made on his behalf by old friend Billy McNeill, who was vacating the job of Clyde manager to become manager of Aberdeen. Brown also retained his second job as a lecturer at Craigie College, and won the old Scottish Second Division in his first season as a manager. More importantly, Brown began to cultivate the characteristics he would later implement with success as Scotland manager. Brown describes the opportunity to coach Clyde's small squad as a delight, and due to the limited resources available it was essential for Brown truly to understand the value of the players in his squad. Brown also overhauled the scouting system at Clyde to ensure value when trading with other clubs. Off the field, the ambitious young manager also demonstrated excellent communication skills and secured a shirt sponsorship deal. In doing so, Clyde became only the second Scottish club to have such a deal after Hibernian.

Brown also developed future Scotland star Steve Archibald at Clyde before selling him on to Aberdeen. Archibald famously went on to sign for Tottenham Hotspur, and to date he is the only Scottish player to play for Spanish giants Barcelona. Brown also developed Pat Nevin, who had been released by Celtic Boys Club for being too small. Nevin became European Youth Player of the Year while with Clyde after starring at the European Under-18 Championship, which Scotland won under the management of Andy Roxburgh. Brown later sold Nevin to Chelsea. In total, Brown managed Clyde from 1977–86, though progression through the Scottish divisions plateaued due to the limited financial resources available at the club.

Brown's credentials had not gone unnoticed at national level, and the SFA had been keen for him to join the Scotland National Team set-up since the early 1980s. In a move typical of Brown's methodical approach, and a career interwoven with the true heavyweights of Scottish football, Brown had previously turned down an offer to become Scotland's assistant manager when Jock Stein was in charge. Brown's rationale was that he felt he did not have quite enough experience for the job at that stage of his career. Interestingly, after the death of Stein, Brown recalls Scottish football journalists' doubts over the authenticity of this story and the job offer. This media doubt over Brown's credentials would later become a prominent theme in the Scottish press and is perhaps why Brown's story remains somewhat overlooked in the annals of Scottish football history.

Stein's sudden death in 1985 rocked Scottish football. As mentioned in the previous chapter, Stein died at Ninian Park, Cardiff, following a 1–1 draw with Wales in the final qualification match for the 1986 World Cup. The draw was enough to see Scotland progress to a two-legged play-off against Australia, which they won 2–0 on aggregate. However, Scottish football still mourned a legend, and Brown describes Stein as a one-off, whose like has never been seen before or since. Even so, Scotland had qualified for the World Cup in Mexico, and Alex Ferguson, who had been assistant manager to Stein, was appointed caretaker manager for the World Cup. Ferguson subsequently asked Brown to become part of his coaching staff to travel to Mexico, and Brown's seemingly inevitable trajectory towards the Scotland National Team set-up was complete. Having been drawn in the World Cup's 'group of death' along with West Germany, Denmark and Uruguay, Scotland exited Mexico 86 in the first round, but Brown states that he returned to Scotland a wiser man.

After Mexico 86, Alex Ferguson was appointed manager of Manchester United and the Scotland job was given to surprise 'Largs Mafia' candidate Andy Roxburgh. In many ways, Roxburgh was a comparable figure to Brown in terms of experience and credentials, and on Roxburgh's appointment Brown was offered the role of Scotland's assistant manager and also manager of the Under-21 team. At the same time, Brown was also offered the opportunity to join the Board of Directors at Rangers. Had he accepted, Brown would have been responsible for development of the apprentices at Ibrox. Instead, he opted for Scotland, and after a successful teaching career he finally handed in his notice at Craigie College and re-entered professional football on a full-time basis.

Brown took charge of the Scotland Under-21s for the first time on 9 September 1986 and steered Scotland to a 1–0 win over West Germany at Ibrox. Kevin Gallacher, who would later become a trusted on-field lieutenant on the France 98 journey, scored the goal. Tom Boyd and Gordon Durie, who also feature strongly in Scotland's World Cup 1998 story, played in this match. Brown also managed Scotland's other age groups during this period, and in 1987 he guided Scotland to the quarter-finals of the Under-18 World Cup in Chile. Of the future France 98 squad, Billy McKinlay featured for the 1987 Under-18s squad. Paul Lambert and John Collins were also selected, but were not released by their clubs, St Mirren and Hibernian respectively! In 1989, Brown also took charge of Scotland as the host nation of the Under-16 World Cup. In what he later described as one of his proudest managerial achievements, Brown steered Scotland's Under-16s to the World Cup Final against Saudi Arabia at Hampden Park on 24 June 1989. In a match attended by over 50,000 people, Scotland came agonisingly close to winning the World Cup on home soil, eventually losing on penalties after extra time, having led the match 2–0.

Despite Brown's promising achievements with Scotland's younger teams, the senior team stuttered at first under Roxburgh and Brown, and were unable to qualify for Euro 88 in West Germany. Next came qualification for the 1990 World Cup in Italy, and Scotland fared better in a difficult group that included a France team featuring Manchester United icon-in-waiting Eric Cantona and future France 98 World Cup captain Didier Deschamps. Both Cantona and Deschamps were on the scoresheet when Scotland were beaten 3–0 by France in Paris on 11 October 1989. Fortunately, this heavy defeat was the low point of the Italy 1990 qualification campaign for Scotland. Mo Johnston, who played for French side Nantes at the beginning of the campaign, was in inspired form throughout qualification, finishing as the group's top scorer on six goals. Famously, by the end of 1989 Johnston's media profile had been raised to an incredible level as he became the first Catholic to sign for Rangers. He also became the first Scottish footballer to require professional bodyguards, after allegedly receiving credible coded death threats from the IRA. In the end, Scotland gained the second automatic qualification spot behind group-winners Yugoslavia and progressed to the 1990 World Cup ahead of France. This disappointing campaign for France cost their coach Henri Michel his job (though as future manager of Morocco, this is not the last we will hear of Michel in Scotland's France 98 story).

Brown later reflects, having been a player at Rangers and Dundee where there were many internationals, that he did not feel out of place in the Scotland dressing room. Despite having won no senior caps, Brown recollects that he was never overawed and was perfectly comfortable working with international footballers, though he later conceded that, even while he was Scotland's assistant manager, he never considered he would one day hold the position of manager. Nonetheless, the 1990 World Cup in Italy was Brown's second World Cup as part of the Scotland set-up, and he was gathering experience of how to build a successful international squad. The 1990 World Cup also gave Brown one of his most painful days in the dugout, as Scotland went down 1–0 to Costa Rica in their opening match in Genoa. Brown later described this match as agony to watch, and despite rallying to a 2–1 victory against Sweden, and almost holding Brazil to a draw, Scotland exited after the first round.

Next for Roxburgh and Brown was Euro 92 qualification, with Scotland drawn in Group Two alongside Switzerland, Romania, Bulgaria and San Marino. With only one qualification spot available for the finals in Sweden, Scotland, impressively, won this tight group with eleven points. Switzerland finished level with Romania on ten points, with Bulgaria only one point behind on nine. In a group characterised by close matches and late goals, Ally McCoist got the knack of finding vital goals at crucial moments, something he did so often throughout his club career at Rangers. It should also not be forgotten that during this campaign the Romania side featured their greatest ever player, Gheorghe Hagi, at his peak with Real Madrid at the time. Bulgaria likewise featured their most legendary star, Hristo Stoichkov, also in the form of his life with Barcelona. Fortunately for Scotland, both players had yet to have their finest international hour, with Bulgaria losing semi-finalists and Romania losing quarter-finalists at the 1994 World Cup in the USA. Stoichkov also finished USA 94 as joint-top scorer with six goals with Russian Oleg Salenko. (Salenko has a Scottish football connection, as he went on to play for Rangers in 1995.)

For Roxburgh and Brown, qualification for Euro 92 in Sweden was a huge achievement, as this was the first time Scotland had made it to the European Championships. During this period, the tournament was only contested by eight countries, with the host nation gaining automatic qualification. Scotland had therefore gained one of only seven available places in the tournament, alongside the other qualification group-winners France, England, CIS (now Russia), Germany, the Netherlands and Denmark. In one of the great football stories, Denmark ultimately triumphed at Euro 92 despite a late call-up as Group Four runners-up, due to wartorn Yugoslavia's late removal from the tournament.

During March and April 1992, Brown also led Scotland's Under-21s to the semi-finals of the European Under-21 Championships. They were eventually eliminated at the final hurdle by Sweden over two legs, but the tournament will best be remembered for Scotland's incredible 5–4 aggregate win over Germany at the quarter-final stage on 24 March in Aberdeen. Captained by Paul Lambert, Scotland were 3–1 down on the night and 4–2 down on aggregate during the second leg, before a late, resounding three-goal comeback at Pittodrie Stadium.

This was an encouraging precursor to the Euro 92 finals in June 1992, and Scotland's final squad for the tournament featured four players Brown would later name in his final 22 for France 98: Gordon Durie, Kevin Gallacher, Tom Boyd and Derek Whyte. Scotland's Euro 92 group also comprised Germany, the Netherlands and the CIS, which Brown later described as the toughest group he had ever experienced. Germany (as West Germany) were reigning world champions, and the Netherlands, featuring AC Milan trio Ruud Gullit, Marco van Basten and Frank Rijkaard, were reigning European champions. At the tournament, Scotland battled bravely but lost 1–0 to the Dutch, following a 75th-minute Dennis Bergkamp strike, and 2–0 to Germany, following goals from Karl-Heinz Riedle and Stefan Effenberg. In the final group match, Scotland convincingly won 3–0 against the CIS, with goals from Paul McStay, Brian McClair and Gary McAllister. As expected, the Netherlands and Germany advanced to the knockout stage.

Brown's increasingly impressive CV now boasted three major tournaments with Scotland, and the qualifiers for USA 94 were his fourth major campaign as assistant manager. Following Euro 92, Roxburgh and Brown embarked on World Cup qualification with renewed confidence, but they got off to the worst possible start with a 3–1 away defeat to Switzerland on 9 September 1992. 0–0 home draws against Italy and Portugal then followed, before a 3–0 home victory versus Malta provided a much-needed win.

Then came Brown's date with destiny, and a match that would dramatically alter the direction of the Scotland National Team and set their trajectory for the next decade. On 28 April 1993, Scotland faced Portugal away in Lisbon. This was the era that saw the emergence of Portugal's 'golden generation' featuring stars such as Luís Figo and Rui Costa, who had won the Under-20 World Cup in 1991, beating Brazil on home soil in a final attended by 127,000 people. Portugal's team to face Scotland blended youth with established performers such as Paulo Futre and Rui Barros, while Scotland went into the game low on confidence.

Parallel to this fixture, Walter Smith's Rangers were also contesting the latter stages of the 1992–93 Champions League, with Scotland's match against Portugal in the same month as Rangers' crucial matches against Olympique de Marseille and CSKA Moscow. Scotland had a strong Rangers contingent at the time, players whom Rangers also relied upon heavily in the Champions League. This was largely because UEFA regulations at the time decreed that clubs could field only three foreign players in European competition. Brown later questioned whether these Rangers players gave their full concentration to the Portugal fixture, while also conceding that these same players were expected to peak several times in quick succession. Either way, Scotland went down 5–0 to Portugal in Lisbon. In what became one of the most disastrous evenings in the history of the Scotland National Team, prolific goalscorer Ally McCoist also suffered a nasty leg break in the match, and sparks flew in several directions in the aftermath.

One particular story gained considerable traction as the dust settled on a miserable night in Lisbon. Scotland had been captained by Rangers' captain Richard Gough on the night, and in *The Game of My Life*, Brown responds to Gough's disclosure that the Scotland team had been told on the eve of the match that midfielder Rui Barros, who ultimately scored two for Portugal in the 5-0 defeat, would not be playing. Brown confirms this occurred, but denies an additional tabloid story that he and Roxburgh received this tip-off from a taxi driver in Lisbon. Brown claims he received the information from former England manager Bobby Robson, then manager of Sporting Lisbon, while travelling back from Scotland's Under-21 fixture against Portugal.

Brown's story, which appears to hold more water, is that Robson advised him the young Luís Figo would start for Portugal on the night in place of Barros. This led to Roxburgh and Brown initially preparing the Scotland team for Figo and then shortly before kick-off informing the team that Barros would indeed be starting after all. Brown states he later clarified with Portugal manager Carlos Queiroz that Barros had failed two urine tests on the lead-up to the match due to taking a course of antibiotics. Robson's tip-off had therefore been accurate when he gave it to Brown, but Barros then passed a late urine test and was drafted back into Portugal's starting eleven.

Despite – or perhaps because of – being an ex-Rangers player himself, a noticeable pattern emerges of Brown experiencing difficulty managing Scotland's Rangers players. It should not be forgotten that Rangers were on course at that time to win their fifth of nine league titles in a row, and players such as McCoist, Gough and Andy Goram had a considerable media profile at the time. Gough and Goram also had an almost telepathic on-field relationship with the fiercely competitive Rangers centre-back John Brown, who played over 200 matches for Rangers during the club's most successful era but never won a Scotland cap, and would undoubtedly be in the reckoning for a defensive place in Scotland's best 'uncapped eleven'. In Portugal, Roxburgh chose to play the injury-prone Craig Levein instead in central defence. Levein then had to be substituted after 60 minutes on that dismal night in Lisbon, and it was no secret that the Rangers contingent felt John Brown should have played instead of Levein.

Roxburgh remained in charge for home and away victories against Estonia, but resigned after the 1-1 draw at home against Switzerland on 8 September 1993 that eliminated Scotland from the 1994 World Cup. Roxburgh's reign was over after 61 matches, and as he stood down he provided the famous quote that his Scotland team had 'died in Portugal'.

It should not be forgotten that Roxburgh was the first Scotland manager to qualify for the Euros, and that he not only raised Scottish coaching standards but also pride in the Scotland National Team. For example, it was he who insisted that the SFA follow suit with Scotland's rugby team by introducing 'Flower of Scotland' as the national anthem over the cheerless 'Scotland the Brave'.

Following Roxburgh's exit, Brown was handed the unenviable task of acting as Scotland's caretaker manager for the penultimate USA 94 qualification match against Italy, in the Olympic Stadium in Rome on 13 October 1993. Italy's team of the era was littered with stars such as Roberto Baggio, Paolo Maldini and Franco Baresi, and Italy would eventually go all the way to the final at USA 94. Scotland, on the other hand, had been eliminated and required a period of reconstruction. The SFA gave themselves six weeks to mull over this unfortunate scenario, and Brown reflects that he felt poorly treated by the SFA at the time, due to the high level of uncertainty around his own Scotland future. In reality, this would be Brown's only match as Scotland's caretaker manager, but he did not know this as he prepared a beleaguered Scotland team for an incredibly difficult away fixture.

In his first big call as Scotland boss, Brown dropped Celtic's Paul McStay for the match against Italy, a decision that created considerable controversy at the time, as McStay had been a media favourite to be handed the captain's armband. In the match itself, Italy raced into a two-goal lead from Roberto Donadoni and Pierluigi Casiraghi within 16 minutes in front of over 60,000 fans in Rome, and Brown recollects he felt an unparalleled numbness and bewilderment in Scotland's dugout, as he feared annihilation at the hands of the Italians. Fortunately for Brown, his Scotland side rallied, and pulled a goal back almost immediately through Kevin Gallacher. Thereafter, Scotland were in the game, and only succumbed to defeat when Stefano Eranio added a third for Italy with ten minutes remaining.

Amid a torrent of media speculation on who would be Scotland's next manager, Brown prepared to enter his second and final match as caretaker against Malta on 17 November 1993. The newspapers ran stories on a multitude of possible candidates such as Kenny Dalglish, Alex Ferguson, Gordon McQueen, Billy Bremner, Joe Jordan and Graeme Souness. Brown recalls he was seldom touted for the job in the media, and he himself was unsure he even wanted the job following the Portugal debacle. Brown therefore concedes he was unprepared for the offer when Jim Farry, SFA Chief Executive at the time, pulled him aside on the eve of the Malta match and offered him the job of Scotland manager up to and including Euro 96. Brown reflects that he felt full of pride to be offered the job and worked out his terms immediately with the SFA. Brown's appointment was met with a round of applause in the Scotland dressing room prior to kick-off, and he subsequently steered Scotland to a 2–0 away victory in his first match as Scotland manager.

Brown's first move as Scotland manager was to appoint Alex Miller, manager of Hibernian at the time, as his assistant. Brown considered Miller a man of integrity who had accumulated deserved widespread respect as a player with Rangers and then as manager of St Mirren and Hibernian. Even so, there is no mistaking that Brown considered himself firmly Scotland's number one and more than qualified to hold the top position. In terms of his management style, Brown describes himself as an autocratic and dogmatic manager, to the point of being dictatorial. Brown recollects his regimes were in no way a democracy, and he would not tolerate any debates about his team selection or tactics. Brown was also a meticulous planner with excruciating attention to detail, characteristics that would be invaluable when planning away trips, training camps and major tournament itineraries. Regardless of their profile or stature, players who crossed Brown rarely found themselves back in his squads, which led to high-profile omissions and generated countless newspaper column inches. Brown in turn resented newspaper polls that rated his appointment as unpopular among a Scottish public who appeared unsure of his credentials.

In the first of chapter of Brown's reign, the omission of Rangers' captain Richard Gough was undoubtedly the biggest media talking point. In the aftermath of the 5–0 defeat in Portugal, Gough had been critical of previous manager Andy Roxburgh, and refused to play for Scotland again while he was in charge. Brown had not forgotten this episode, and when Gough then announced he would be available to play for Scotland following Roxburgh's departure, Brown had other ideas. Controversially, Brown decided Gough would no longer be picked for Scotland, and then did not relent when faced with a media onslaught and huge unpopularity among Rangers supporters. Brown always cited football reasons for his decision to omit Gough permanently. However, it is possible that Brown simply disliked Gough's treatment of Roxburgh and thought Gough had disrespected the Scotland National Team.

Gough was not the only high-profile Rangers player whose international career came to a premature conclusion under Brown. Indeed, history suggests two worlds collided when Brown was appointed Scotland boss, with his international regime at odds with the Rangers 'nine in a row' culture from the outset. Later, at the conclusion of the 1997–98 season, Brown's resistance to blending Scotland's experienced Rangers players with Celtic's new wave, led by Paul Lambert and Craig Burley, perhaps cost Brown the opportunity to take Scotland into uncharted territory when the stakes were at their very highest.

The Euro 96 qualifiers were Brown's first major tournament campaign as Scotland manager, and the prize for success would be a treasured spot at the finals in England. Brown's Scotland began the campaign on 7 September 1994 in a tricky away fixture against group rivals Finland. Scotland emerged as 2–0 victors in Helsinki, with goals from Duncan Shearer and John Collins, and this important win set the tone for what would prove to be an excellent first qualifying campaign for Brown. In a group eventually won by Russia on 26 points, Scotland comfortably achieved automatic qualification in second place on 23 points, five points ahead of third-placed Greece.

During this campaign, Brown also demonstrated shrewd tactical awareness in implementing the 3–5–2 formation to great effect. In *Inverting the Pyramid*, Jonathan Wilson credits the creation of the 3–5–2 to Carlos Bilardo, Argentina's head coach at the 1986 World Cup. Wilson dispels the myth that the mercurial Diego Maradona won the 1986 World Cup single-handedly with his account of Bilardo's deliberations on how he would fit Argentina's little genius into a team. The result was the 3–5–2, unseen before Mexico 86 but by Italia 90 the formation of choice for several nations, including eventual winners West Germany.

Brown was convinced that the 3–5–2 played to Scotland's strengths, and West Germany's World Cup success with the formation had inspired Brown to test the system with the Scotland Under-21 team in 1992. During this period, Brown did not use the term 'wing-back', instead referring to his 'wide midfielders', whom he instructed to prioritise defensive duties but support the attack when needed. Of the three centre-backs, Brown considered one as the 'free defender', who would be the most comfortable on the ball. This formation later served Brown in every match of the France 98 journey, and became second nature to his first eleven, regardless of who was picked to play. Interestingly, in the final crucial matches of Scotland's successful Euro 2020 qualification under manager Steve Clarke, which ended 22 years of qualification failure, Clarke also unexpectedly deployed the 3–5–2 formation, having previously favoured a four-man defence.

Scotland's Euro 96 adventure is now mainly remembered for the epic group stage encounter against England at Wembley on the 15 June 1996. In a tight battle, England took the lead on 53 minutes through Alan Shearer. However, Scotland were famously handed a lifeline on 78 minutes after Tony Adams tripped Gordon Durie in the box. Gary McAllister, who had been successful from the spot four years earlier versus the CIS at Euro 92, stepped up to take the vital penalty for Scotland. Unfortunately for Scotland, this time England's excellent goalkeeper David Seaman saved McAllister's crucial spot kick. This routine footballing event took on a bizarre dimension when it later emerged that famous spoon-bender Uri Geller was flying above Wembley in a helicopter in what he claimed was an attempt to use his paranormal abilities to affect play on the pitch below. Some commentators noted that on slow-motion replays the ball did indeed appear to move of its own accord just before McAllister struck it. Whatever the true cause of the penalty miss, what was certain was that, only moments later, Paul Gascoigne, a Rangers player at the time, scored his only England goal at a major international tournament with an inspired piece of skill and finish past his clubmate Andy Goram.

Overall, Brown's side gave an excellent account of themselves at Euro 96, and came agonisingly close to progression from the group stages. Scotland finished the group stages on identical points and goal difference to a Dutch team containing stars like Edwin van der Sar, Edgar Davids, Clarence Seedorf, Patrick Kluivert and Dennis Bergkamp. Having drawn 0–0 at Villa Park, Birmingham, 'goals for' were used as the tiebreaker to separate the two sides. The Netherlands therefore emerged from the group courtesy of a 78th-minute Kluivert consolation strike in a 4–1 mauling from England at Wembley in their final group match on 18 June, a match in which Alan Shearer, eventual top scorer in the tournament with five goals, and strike partner Teddy

Sheringham each grabbed two goals. Scotland had defeated Switzerland 1–0 at Villa Park on the same evening thanks to a 36th-minute Ally McCoist strike, and until Kluivert's goal Scotland held the second automatic qualification spot behind group-winners England. Nonetheless, the victory over Switzerland provided Scotland with an extremely respectable but ultimately insufficient tally of four points from a tough group.

3

BROWN'S INVERTED PYRAMID

On 31 August 1996, just eight weeks after the conclusion of Euro 96, Scotland lined up against Austria in a tough France 98 qualification opener. Scotland's first starting eleven saw Craig Brown make only one change from the side that had defeated Switzerland at Euro 96, with Everton striker Duncan Ferguson replacing Gordon Durie. Ferguson had not been part of Brown's Euro 96 squad, but had been part of Andy Roxburgh's squad for the 1992 European Championships four years earlier when he was just 20 years old. In 1992, Ferguson had become one of the few players to represent Scotland at the Euros, coming off the bench to replace Manchester United's Brian McClair in Scotland's group opener against the Netherlands.

This France 98 qualifier in Austria over four years later would turn out to be one of only seven Scotland caps won by Ferguson in total, with no goals scored – surprisingly few, perhaps, given that this tall and powerful striker later established himself in England's Premier League and won the FA Cup with Everton in 1995. Unfortunately, Ferguson also received a three-month prison sentence in October 1995 after being found guilty of assaulting Raith Rovers player John McStay on the pitch in 1994. This forgettable incident occurred during Ferguson's ill-fated spell with Rangers, following his promising £4 million British record move in 1993 from Dundee United. During France 98 qualification, Ferguson featured in only one other match, which was his last for Scotland, and he was not part of Brown's final squad for the tournament, having retired from international football before the end of the campaign. During a long and successful career in the English top flight, Ferguson proved he was a striker capable of scoring at the highest level, a commodity Scotland did not possess in abundance during this period.

In this first France 98 qualification match, Scotland ultimately drew 0–0 with Austria in the Ernst Happel Stadion, Vienna, in a performance Brown summarised as 'professional and pleasing'. Although Austria had not qualified for Euro 96, the 1994 World Cup or Euro 92, they provided organised opposition and had retained key players with major tournament experience gained at the 1990 World Cup. In terms of chances created, Rangers favourite Ally McCoist came closest to opening the scoring with a low, right-footed strike from just outside the box in the first half. Ferguson also came close to breaking the deadlock with a header in the last minute after good work on the left by John Collins. Had Ferguson scored this header, such are the fine margins of football at the elite level that perhaps his Scotland career might have played out differently. Nonetheless, this away draw would later prove to be an important point won in the overall context of the group.

Scotland's next fixture of the campaign was against Latvia at the Daugavas Stadion, Riga, on 5 October 1996. This was Scotland's first match against Latvia following their regained independence after the collapse of the Soviet Union in 1990. Since then, Latvia had also competed in the qualification phases of the 1994 World Cup and Euro 96. Though they had qualified for neither tournament, they had managed a respectable four victories during Euro 96 qualification. In later years, Latvia reached the Euro 2004 finals in Portugal, their only major finals appearance to date, but in 1996 it was inconceivable that Scotland could come unstuck in such a fixture.

The Scotland side Brown named to face Latvia contained four changes from the previous match against Austria. Middlesbrough's Derek Whyte replaced Blackburn Rovers' Colin Hendry in central defence, and John Spencer of Chelsea and Darren Jackson of Hibernian replaced Duncan Ferguson and Ally McCoist. Scotland took the lead after 18 minutes with a fantastic left-footed strike from John Collins. Collins, an outstanding midfield player and favourite of manager Brown's, had recently joined French Division 1 club AS Monaco from Celtic. In trademark style, Collins had evidently worked on the training pitch with Gary McAllister and Rangers' Stuart McCall for the set-piece free kick that resulted in the goal. After using McAllister as a decoy, Collins swivelled onto his favoured left foot and smashed a shot from 25 yards past Latvia goalkeeper Olegs Karavajevs. A truly spectacular and perhaps somewhat forgotten Scotland goal, Collins' thunderbolt was vital in setting Scotland on a positive trajectory towards France 98 qualification. Scotland had to wait until the 80th minute before finding a decisive second goal. This was Darren Jackson's first international goal, a well-taken sidefooted strike from outside the box after Jackson had showed good skill to capitalise on a slack pass that left the Latvian back line exposed. So Brown's Scotland emerged from this tricky encounter in Riga as 2–0 away victors, and with four points from a possible six.

Scotland were scheduled to face Estonia in Tallinn four days later on 9 October 1996, in what turned out to be one of the most bizarre episodes in the history of the Scotland National Team. Scotland arrived at the Kadriorg Stadium in the Estonian capital the day before the match. On inspection of the stadium facilities, the Scottish delegation were concerned about unbalanced lighting from temporary floodlights, which seemingly created glare and made the ball hard to see in certain areas of the pitch. The concerns were apparently shared by FIFA's match delegate Jean-Marie Gantenbein, leading to Scotland filing a complaint to FIFA headquarters in Zurich. FIFA held an emergency late-night meeting, and decided the scheduled 6.45pm kick-off would be moved to 3pm to avoid the requirement for floodlights. Common sense had prevailed.

Or had it? Apparently not! *FourFourTwo* later reported that the Estonian Football Association were aggrieved by FIFA's decision, claiming they would lose revenue and could not manage the logistics of this late change. On 9 October, Scotland duly took to the field fully kitted and prepared to play the match at 3pm, but there were no Estonians. Estonia's coach, Icelandic Tietur Thordarson, refused to budge on the original kick-off time, leading to referee Miroslav Radoman commencing the match with only Scotland's eleven players on the pitch. Radoman then blew for full-time three seconds later, and Brown's men left the pitch and returned to the changing rooms.

Approximately 600 bemused Scotland supporters were present in Tallinn, having been made aware of the early kick-off by members of the official SFA delegation patrolling streets and bars. Famously, the Tartan Army kept up spirits with choruses of 'Only one team in Tallinn!' Some then took to the pitch for a quick kickabout as the afternoon descended into chaos. As Brown's squad were leaving the Kadriorg Stadium, the Estonian team bus then arrived, with Scotland seemingly now assured by Gantenbein that the fixture had been forfeited and Scotland would receive a 3–0 walkover result.

But the story was far from over. Amazingly, a FIFA committee then met a month later and decided a rematch must be played at a neutral venue, rescheduling the fixture for 11 February 1997 in Monaco. FIFA's decision caused much frustration for Scotland, as Estonia had chosen to ignore a FIFA ruling direct from Zurich, with few apparent consequences. The Scotland eleven who turned out in the cancelled fixture in Tallinn also did not win international caps.

With Hampden Park unavailable due to renovation work, all of Scotland's home qualifying matches for France 98 were scheduled to take place at alternative venues. The first would see Craig Brown's men face a stern test against Sweden at Ibrox Stadium on 10 November 1996. At the previous World Cup in 1994, Sweden had finished in a surprise third place in the USA, falling at the semi-final stage 1–0 to eventual winners Brazil. Surprisingly, Sweden did not follow up their remarkable achievement at USA 94 during Euro 96 qualification, failing to qualify for the finals in England from a group won by Switzerland, with Turkey in second place. But concerningly for Scotland, Sweden's squad still featured most of the stars from their USA 94 heroics. In fact, five of the Swedish starting line-up to face Scotland at Ibrox had started the World Cup semi-final in front of 91,500 fans at the Rose Bowl, Pasadena on 13 July 1994. Stefan Schwartz of Fiorentina and Jesper Blomqvist of Serie A rivals Milan, starters at Ibrox for this match, were also unused World Cup semi-final substitutes. Future Celtic icon Henrik Larsson, then of Dutch side Feyenoord, was a substitute for both matches. Kennet Andersson of Serie A side Bologna started the World Cup semi-final, but was a substitute at Ibrox. In Tommy Svensson, Sweden had also retained their USA 94 manager.

Scotland's team on the night saw Celtic's Jackie McNamara win his first cap, and the introduction of Bolton's John McGinlay to play in a lone striker role. Darren Jackson also held his place, to provide the hard running to support both McGinlay up front and a midfield three of John Collins, Craig Burley, still at this point a Chelsea player, and Blackburn Rovers' Billy McKinlay. As discussed in the preceding chapter, manager Brown deployed his favoured 3–5–2, utilising McNamara and Celtic's Tosh McKinlay as wing-backs. In defence, Tottenham Hotspur's Colin Calderwood and Celtic's Tom Boyd played either side of the increasingly influential Colin Hendry in the back three.

The match itself was one the most memorable in the modern history of the Scotland National Team, with Ibrox providing a cauldron of energy for the occasion. After tight opening exchanges, Scotland made the perfect start to the match on seven minutes. Tom Boyd picked up the ball deep on the left and was not closed down by Sweden's midfield, allowing him to play a searching diagonal ball towards the feet of Darren Jackson, who had dropped into an advanced central midfield position. In a moment of inspiration, Jackson perfectly gauged the pace of the pass from Boyd and dummied the ball. Jackson's dummy completely fooled the Swedish defence, but striker McGinlay read the situation, latching onto the pass with an excellent left-footed first touch, which created the space to allow him deftly to dispatch the ball past experienced goalkeeper Thomas Ravelli with his right. The goal sent the Tartan Army, already in fine voice, into raptures in the stands. For Sweden, this was a nightmare start, as Brown's Scotland were an organised and hardworking side who conceded few goals.

On 16 minutes, Sweden then suffered an injury to lone striker Martin Dahlin, which altered the complexion of the match. Dahlin, who days earlier had returned to former club Borussia Mönchengladbach on loan during an ill-fated spell as an AS Roma player, had shown little to worry Hendry and Calderwood in the early stages, but his injury led to the introduction of Kennet Andersson. At 6ft 4in (1.93m), Andersson was a more awkward proposition for the Scottish defence to handle, and had netted an incredible five goals at World Cup 94, finishing in the illustrious company of Roberto Baggio, Jürgen Klinsmann and Romário as tied second-top scorer.

For the remainder of the first half, Sweden's Schwartz and Jonas Thern dominated the midfield, and fed wingers Blomqvist and Niclas Alexandersson to provide crosses for substitute Andersson. Blomqvist, who had just made his big-money move from IFK Gothenburg to Milan, looked particularly dangerous on the left wing. Two seasons later,

Blomqvist would win the treble with Manchester United, and was a starter in the Nou Camp when Manchester United dramatically defeated Bayern Munich to secure the Champions League.

Despite Sweden's first-half dominance, Scotland preserved their slender 1–0 lead until half time, though Sweden had come close to an equaliser just before the break, when Andersson passed up a golden chance from a free header, following an Alexandersson cross from the right.

Craig Brown withdrew debutant McNamara at half time, following the 23-year-old landing awkwardly on his shoulder after a good attacking run on the right wing late in the first half. Paul Lambert was McNamara's replacement, with the versatile Craig Burley switching to right wing-back for the second half. Lambert, who had not made Scotland's Euro 96 squad, had impressed in a pre-season trial with Borussia Dortmund, and had made his debut in the Bundesliga three months earlier in August 1996. The 1996–97 season would end with incredible personal achievement for Lambert when he became the first British player of the Champions League era to win the trophy after his side beat Juventus 3–1 in Munich, and the first British player to win the trophy with a non-UK club.

The second half saw Sweden increase the pressure on Brown's Scotland. In response, captain Hendry marshalled Scotland's defence, alongside the equally impressive Calderwood. It was evident by now that Scotland were up against an excellent team, but Brown's men were able to stand resolute in the face of wave after wave of Swedish pressure. Jim Leighton, still a Hibs players at this point and winning his 75th international cap, put together an incredible string of saves in the second half that won him the Man of the Match award. Scotland ultimately stood firm and frustrated their talented opponents. The 1–0 win meant Scotland had taken seven points from a possible nine in their first three qualifiers.

Scotland's fourth match of the campaign was the rescheduled away fixture on 11 February 1997 against Estonia, the second instalment of the aforementioned farce that had begun in Tallinn the previous October. This match was to take place at the neutral Stade Louis II Stadium in Monaco, with Craig Brown fielding a more attacking set-up than against Sweden. On the night, Andy Goram returned as goalkeeper and Duncan Ferguson made his seventh and final Scotland appearance alongside John McGinlay in attack. Paul McStay was also introduced in midfield for the first time during the campaign. The experienced McStay spent his entire club career with Celtic, making over 500 appearances for the Parkhead club. McStay was winning his 74th cap of a 76-cap international career.

Scotland were undeniably the better team on the night and created chances, at least one of which should have been converted. Unfortunately for Brown's men, they faced an in-form Estonian goalkeeper in Mart Poom. Poom, then of Derby County, went on to play 137 times in the English Premier League, and was capped 120 times in an 18-year international career. Scotland's best opportunity of the night fell to defender Tom Boyd, who rattled the crossbar in the first half with a left-footed strike after a flying header from Gary McAllister had been blocked. Ferguson was also thwarted by Poom in the first half when freed to shoot inside the box after McStay, John Collins and McAllister had combined well. The farcical circumstances of this fixture bore all the hallmarks of a preordained slip-up and a loss of vital qualification points for Scotland. This proved to be the case, with Scotland unable to break down Estonia in a forgettable 0–0 draw, and booed from the pitch by a Tartan Army by then accustomed to major tournament qualification. Despite the circumstances that had led to the rematch, Brown later acknowledged that it was a poor Scotland performance.

Scotland's next match was against Estonia at home at Rugby Park, Kilmarnock, on 29 March 1997, with the stadium hosting its first international match for 80 years. Jim Leighton returned as goalkeeper, in what was becoming a dual with Andy Goram of Rangers for the number one spot. This would later develop into a major news story on the eve of France 98, and provide a controversial end to the talented Goram's 43-cap international career.

The team also saw three outfield changes, with Tosh McKinlay, Darren Jackson and Scot Gemmill of Nottingham Forest replacing Jackie McNamara, John McGinlay and John Collins, who was suspended after receiving a second booking of the campaign. Gemmill, son of Archie Gemmill, scorer of Scotland's most famous World Cup goal, against the Netherlands at Argentina 78 – now almost as legendary for its part in the 1996 film *Trainspotting* – was winning his seventh cap. Due to the debacle in Tallinn and the eventual loss of valuable points, SFA President Bill Dickie requested in the match programme that the Tartan Army respect the Estonian national anthem, and avoid any expression of ill-feeling toward the Estonian FA. Plaudits were also given beforehand to Kilmarnock FC physio Hugh Allan, who was celebrating an incredible 210 consecutive caps as a physiotherapist with the National Team. In 1997, Allan's caps had already spanned 24 years and included five World Cups and the Euros twice, an incredible feat that will surely never be equalled within Scotland's National Team set-up.

The match kicked off at 3pm on a windy Saturday in Kilmarnock in front of an 18,000-capacity crowd. Brown's Scotland opened nervously, with an awkward and direct Estonian side finding room to break on the flanks. The best chance of the opening exchanges fell to 18-year-old Kristen Viikmäe, who broke clear from the right wing after Scotland had given the ball away cheaply. With time and space, Viikmäe found himself one-on-one with goalkeeper Jim Leighton. Fortunately for Scotland, Leighton's trademark speed off his line caused Viikmäe to rush a lob, which the goalkeeper caught easily. But it was an early warning for Scotland that Estonia would not go down without a fight.

Captain Gary McAllister rallied Scotland and began to control the midfield. Next to McAllister, the steady and assured McStay showed his experience and class, which allowed the less experienced Gemmill to grow into the game. Tosh McKinlay was also in fine form on the left, with Kevin Gallacher and Darren Jackson's usual hard running unsettling the Estonians.

On 25 minutes, Scotland broke the deadlock with a move that deserved a goal. As Scotland moved forward, McStay found Gallacher in space in the left channel, and Gallacher played a superb pass to Tosh McKinlay, who bombed down the left flank. Moving at speed, McKinlay initially carried the ball, then checked back and dummied, confusing the Estonian defender and creating the half a yard he required to cross superbly. The cross found its way to Tom Boyd in space in the box, who drilled a right-footed shot goalwards. Mart Poom made yet another fine save in the Estonian goal, but he could only parry the ball towards Gemmill, who lunged with Estonian defender Marek Lemsalu, causing the ball to bounce in the air for the onrushing Boyd to meet with his head for his first international goal in 42 caps. It was a great moment for Boyd, who had come so close to his first international goal against Estonia in Monaco.

Scotland were now in control and, ironically, when he had waited so long to open his international account, Boyd almost scored a second goal a few minutes later, after he was freed following a clever backheel by Jackson. Collecting the ball in space, Boyd took a touch and fired another great strike goalwards. On this occasion, a desperate block from Estonian defender Sergei Hohlov-Simson sent the ball looping over goalkeeper Poom and it struck the crossbar, in what was the final significant moment of the first half.

Immediately after the restart, disaster almost struck for Scotland, following a collective loss of concentration that culminated in Estonia winning a free kick in a dangerous position on the edge of Scotland's 18-yard box. Martin Reim stepped up for Estonia and struck a terrific shot that seemed netbound all the way, but ultimately crashed against the crossbar, with Leighton possibly getting the slightest of touches on the ball to rescue Scotland. Following a similar pattern to the first-half action, this scare seemed to give Brown's side the jolt they required to play their best football, and Scotland netted the second decisive goal on 52 minutes.

Again, Tosh McKinlay was involved on the left, after being freed by a McAllister pass. This time McKinlay's cross split Jackson and Gemmill, and the move initially broke down, allowing the Estonian defence to clear. To the delight of the Tartan Army, Boyd immediately won back the ball in a dangerous position, which kept the momentum with Scotland. The Estonian back line had not recovered from the initial attack, and Boyd's left-footed cross was heading for Jackson until a clear push in the box by Lemsalu. A penalty shout was academic, as the referee played Scotland's advantage, and Janek Meet sliced his clearance into his own net under pressure from Gallacher. The own goal finally put some daylight between Scotland and the tricky Estonians, and after this goal Scotland showed professionalism in seeing out the match safely, with McAllister and McStay dictating the midfield. To their credit, Estonia did not give up until the final whistle was blown, and Leighton was the busier of the two goalkeepers in the latter stages, having to make two fine saves before the end. Scotland rode their luck slightly, but overall they merited their 2–0 victory on the day.

Scotland's sixth fixture of the France 98 qualification campaign came just four days later on 2 April 1997, a crucial home match against Austria at Celtic Park. Craig Brown made two changes to the team that faced Estonia, with John Collins returning from suspension to replace Scot Gemmill, and Paul Lambert replacing Paul McStay to win his fifth cap. Both Gemmill and McStay had played well against Estonia and might have considered themselves unlucky to be left out against Austria. Stalwart Jim Leighton was winning his 77th cap to join Alex McLeish in joint-second place behind Kenny Dalglish as Scotland's most capped player. Dalglish, Scotland's most decorated footballer, won 102 caps between 1971 and 1986.

Austria's danger men were easily identified as captain

Toni Polster of FC Köln, Austria's record goalscorer with 34 goals, and Andi Herzog of Werder Bremen, who had by now scored vital qualification winners against both Sweden and Latvia. Another known quantity was centre-back Wolfgang Feiersinger, who was also a clubmate of Paul Lambert's at Borussia Dortmund.

After tight opening exchanges, Scotland began to trouble Austria as the first half progressed, with Kevin Gallacher looking particularly bright and sharp. Gallacher was by now an experienced international player, having won his first Scotland cap in 1988 while with Dundee United. In recent matches, Gallacher had developed a good understanding with Darren Jackson, and Jackson's speed and clever play was also increasingly troubling the Austrian defence as the first half wore on. Lambert was also looking like a perfect fit in the Scottish midfield, collecting the ball from centre-backs Colin Hendry and Colin Calderwood in deep positions, and linking the play with a superb range of passing. It was now evident that Lambert had progressed significantly as a player with Dortmund, and that Craig Brown was now capitalising on Lambert's unexpected club form at international level.

On 24 minutes, Scotland took the lead their positive play deserved. This followed the breakdown of an Austrian move on the Scottish right wing, which led to a long diagonal clearance from Tom Boyd. Boyd's clearance was met poorly by Feiersinger, whose header went straight to Gallacher, who capitalised on the loose ball with a superb first-time pass that released Jackson. Jackson's speed caught out the Austrian defence and he raced clear in the left channel and shot with his left foot from a narrow angle. Goalkeeper Michael Konsel parried the shot, but Jackson did not give up, making it to the touchline to steal in behind Konsel with the ball remaining loose. Konsel then appeared to foul Jackson by pulling him back, and Feiersinger made a desperate lunging tackle in an effort to prevent the uncontainable Jackson from netting the rebound. Feiersinger did reach the ball, but was only successful in perfectly teeing up Gallacher, who smashed the ball home with his left foot from six yards.

One-nil to Scotland and deservedly so, but, encouragingly, Scotland did not rest on their laurels before half time. Collins and McAllister were now asserting themselves in midfield, and Jackson's pace was troubling his marker Peter Schöttel. Every time the ball reached the feet of Jackson in an attacking position, he looked likely to roll Schöttel and outstrip him with his speed. This led to two almost identical, cynical fouls by Schöttel on Jackson in quick succession. Schöttel received a yellow card for the first of these fouls, but Russian referee Nikolai Levnikov was extremely lenient on Schöttel the second time round, to the dismay of the Tartan Army, and he brandished no second yellow or red card, when a sending-off had seemed inevitable. Unsurprisingly, Schöttel was substituted at half time, having been given an absolutely torrid time by a Darren Jackson in the form of his life. Although the Austrians had played some neat football in the first half, Scotland had blown them away with an intensity they could not match, and 1–0 at half time perhaps flattered the Austrians. Even so, at 1–0 the match remained on a knife edge.

Scotland emerged for the second half on this cold April night to roars of encouragement from the Tartan Army, who sensed they might be witnessing a memorable night for the Scotland National Team. Immediately, Scotland asserted themselves once more, with Collins, after good combination play with Tosh McKinlay, creating space for a right-footed shot that Konsel saved. Then, a scare for Scotland, as Austria's right back Markus Schopp broke clear on the right wing after some neat football by the Austrians on the halfway line. Tom Boyd raced back with Schopp, but could not catch him, instead making a risky slide tackle as Schopp entered Scotland's penalty box. The stadium fell silent as referee Levnikov blew for a foul, and Scottish hearts sank as they waited for Levnikov to point to the spot for a penalty. To the dismay of the Austrians, Levnikov instead gave a foul less than a yard outside the Scotland penalty box, and the TV replays showed the referee had made the correct decision. The Austrians complained bitterly, and the Tartan Army instantly forgave the Russian referee for his reluctance to send off defender Schöttel in the first half. World Cup qualification campaigns can be decided on fine margins such as these, and fortune was with Brown's Scotland on this occasion.

From the resultant free kick, the disappointed Austrians gave the ball away cheaply, and Scotland countered quickly, a real feature of Scotland's play on the night. Again, Jackson was freed, and this time he beat Feiersinger with his pace, leading to yet another cynical body check on Jackson by Feiersinger. In what looked to be a choice for the referee between a red or yellow card for Feiersinger, unbelievably Levnikov produced no card or even gave a foul, and played on, as he appeared to compensate for denying Austria a penalty only moments earlier. However the official's decisions might have been influencing the game, Scotland continued to look the more dangerous side as they bravely pressed for a second goal rather than defending their slender lead. This allowed Austria to counter, and Leighton was called into action after neat work from danger men Herzog and Polster freed substitute Ivica Vastić in the

Scotland penalty area. In familiar fashion, Leighton was quick off his line to narrow the shooting angle, and the veteran goalkeeper got two strong hands on Vastić's right-footed effort to parry the shot to safety.

On 72 minutes Scotland got the second goal this excellent display merited, and in terms of quality it was one of the best Scotland goals of the modern era. The passage of play started with a throw-in from an advanced position on the right, taken by Craig Burley, who was by now a mainstay of the team at right wing-back. Burley found Gallacher with the throw-in. Though Gallacher could not unshackle himself from Feiersinger, who won the ball, the Austrian's following clearance was aimless and handed the advantage back to Scotland, as the impressive Lambert superbly controlled the ball. Lambert drove Scotland forward, looking for the feet of substitute McGinlay with a pass into the penalty box. Defender Andreas Heraf read the danger and got a strong foot on Lambert's pass, but the deflection sent the ball looping towards Gallacher, who was positioned on the 18-yard line at the corner of the Austrian penalty box. Gallacher controlled the ball brilliantly with his chest and allowed the ball to bounce once. From an unlikely scoring position, he then swivelled his body and struck an incredible diagonal volley which rocketed into the top-left corner of the Austrian net. Konsel must have known immediately it was unsaveable and did not even dive, which perhaps made the goal look even better. It was a great moment for Gallacher, a player Craig Brown had come to rely on in the Scotland attack. Scotland thereafter coasted to a 2–0 victory in this vital match, and captain Gary McAllister described their performance as the best of his international career so far in a post-match interview.

The Group Four table after this victory made pleasant

reading for the Scots. Fourteen points from six matches placed Scotland clearly first in the group, seven points ahead of Austria in second place and eight ahead of Sweden, though both had two games in hand over Scotland. Perhaps the most striking statistic was that Scotland had not yet conceded a goal, achieving six straight clean sheets. Post-match, there was an air of triumphalism among the Scottish media and fans, as it now seemed inconceivable Scotland could let qualification for France 98 slip from this position. Craig Brown, however, had been in football long enough to know this was not the moment to get carried away. In his post-match interview, Brown described the situation as 'far from over'. He pointed out that, while Scotland had dropped four points so far compared to Austria's five, Scotland still had to play Sweden away, while Austria would face the same side at home. Prophetically, Brown recommended that fan and media euphoria be kept in check. If Scotland were to lose to Sweden but Austria defeated the Swedes, then Austria would be in pole position in Group Four.

Scotland's seventh match of the campaign, four weeks later on 30 April 1997, was indeed against Sweden in Gothenburg. Unsurprisingly, following the excellent recent performance against Austria, Craig Brown picked the same team to face the Swedes. There was little doubt that this fixture presented Scotland's sternest test so far, as Sweden, although defeated on the night, had largely outplayed Scotland in Glasgow the previous November. This time, Sweden started with two strikers in Martin Dahlin, still in his loan-back spell at Borussia Mönchengladbach, and Kennet

Andersson, who had caused Scotland so many problems in the reverse fixture at Ibrox.

In Gothenburg, Scotland again had difficulty coming to terms with a talented and physical Sweden team. In the second minute of the match, Sweden went close after right-back Gary Sundgren freed Andreas Andersson on the right wing with a long searching pass. Andersson raced onto the ball and struck a powerful right-footed shot, which Jim Leighton appeared to save. Famous Italian referee Pierluigi Collina thought differently and gave a goal kick, causing protests from the Swedes. This was an early warning shot for the Scots and set the tone for the match.

The early passages of play saw Colin Hendry give away three free kicks within shooting range of the Scotland goal, as he tussled with his nemesis of the France 98 qualification phase, Kennet Andersson. Fortunately for Hendry and Scotland, Sweden spurned all three chances. With the game being played mostly in the air, Scotland's Gary McAllister, John Collins and Paul Lambert attempted to take control of the midfield, but were limited to glimpses of neat play, mostly linked by the tireless running and skilful touches of Kevin Gallacher. As the first half progressed, Scotland grew further into the match, but Sweden continued to look the more dangerous side when moving forwards. On the half-hour mark, Leighton was beaten after a well-worked corner deceived the Scotland defence, and Dahlin shot on the turn from ten yards. On this occasion, the Tartan Army breathed a sigh of relief as Lambert, sticking to his far-post position, cleared off the line.

But this only delayed the inevitable, and Sweden broke the deadlock on 43 minutes. The goal followed more direct play from the Swedes, with the ball hoisted forwards and met by the head of Dahlin. Unusually, Hendry was beaten in the air this time, and the ball bounced once before Kennet Andersson unleashed an unstoppable volley past Leighton. It was a great finish, and the first goal conceded by Scotland in France 98 qualification. Scotland welcomed the half-time whistle against difficult opposition.

Unfortunately for Scotland, the second half followed the pattern of the first, with Kennet Andersson and Dahlin causing all sorts of problems for Scotland's three centre-backs Hendry, Calderwood and Boyd. Darren Jackson, uncontainable by recent opposition, was also kept quiet and unable to disturb Sweden's rhythm. On 63 minutes, Scotland gave the ball away cheaply in midfield, and Dahlin collected and perfectly fed strike partner Kennet Andersson, who controlled the ball, outmanoeuvred Calderwood and fired a low shot past Leighton from 18 yards.

It was 2–0 to Sweden and Craig Brown's Scotland had a mountain to climb. They might have benefitted from substitutions before the hour mark with the score only 1–0, but now the manager acted immediately, replacing Jackson with Gordon Durie and Tosh McKinlay with Scot Gemmill. With all having looked lost for Scotland, the impact of Durie off the bench for Scotland was immediate. Durie began chasing down every ball, and noticeably disrupted the Swedish flow and control of the match. Scotland were two down, but it seemed nobody had told Durie, and his instant impact galvanised Scotland, who thereafter dominated the match and clawed a goal back on 83 minutes after Gallacher headed home from a McAllister corner. Two minutes later, Gallacher was bumped in the box by Patrik Andersson after a quick and clever throw-in from Durie caught out the Swedes, who were now rattled by Scotland's late rally. Gallacher was clearly fouled and stumbled forwards, but opted to stay on his feet. This left Collina with no option but to play on, and Sweden scraped over the finishing line with a 2–1 victory. Gallacher later reflected in Archie Macpherson's *Adventures in the Golden Age* that he was too honest on this occasion, but this is only half of the story, as the shrewd Gallacher learned from this error of judgement, opting to go down in the box the next time against Brazil. The Sweden defeat was a blow to the Scots and left automatic qualification hopes hanging in the balance.

Scotland's eighth and ninth matches of the campaign were home and away matches against Belarus, another nation which gained its independence in 1991 following the collapse of the Soviet Union. The away fixture came first on 8 June 1997, in what was the first ever match contested by the two nations. Scotland travelled to Minsk with injury worries, with Colin Hendry and John Collins replaced in the starting line-up by Derby County's Christian Dailly and David Hopkin of Crystal Palace. Craig Brown later summarised this match as an uneventful but hardworking away win, which was decided by a 50th-minute Gary McAllister penalty, after Darren Jackson was blatantly chopped down in the Belarus penalty area. It was moderate redemption for McAllister after his Euro 96 Wembley nightmare.

The home match against Belarus created an unforeseen moral dilemma for Craig Brown and the SFA, as the fixture was originally scheduled for 6 September 1997, which transpired to be the same day as the funeral of Diana, Princess of Wales. The Princess had been killed in a horror car crash exactly one week earlier, causing national mourning across the Home Nations. Brown was left with the impossible task of speaking to the press and surmising whether or not the home fixture versus Belarus would go ahead. With no funeral announcement yet made, Brown stated in a TV interview that he had not been told of any postponement, which was to the best of the limited knowledge available to him. To Brown's dismay, the funeral date was then announced a short time later on the same date as the match. Ally McCoist phoned Brown immediately and stated he would not play on that date. Rangers clubmates Andy Goram and Gordon Durie backed McCoist, and Brown also spoke to Colin Hendry on the phone, who advised that several other members of the squad shared the same sentiments. In *The Game of My Life* Brown later described feeling misquoted, but ultimately the SFA sought advice from Buckingham Palace, and it was agreed the match would be held a day later on Sunday 7 September 1997.

The overshadowed match ended in an impressive 4–1 victory for Scotland at Pittodrie Stadium, Aberdeen. Kevin Gallacher continued his impressive scoring run with a double, taking him to five goals in the campaign. David Hopkin also grabbed a superb unexpected double after coming on as a 50th-minute substitute for the injured Gary McAllister.

Scotland entered their final match of the campaign on 20 points. By this point, Austria had 22 points and were expected to beat Belarus at home in their final match, which they later did, 4–0, to win the group on 25 points. Scotland's target was to finish as best second-placed nation across the nine groups, which was calculated by points won against the first, third and fourth nations in each group – Austria, Sweden and Latvia in Scotland's case. Scotland already had 13 points from these fixtures with only Latvia left for them to play again. Only Spain could claim the automatic runner-up spot ahead of Scotland, and only in the unlikely event that the Spaniards lost to the Faroe Islands and themselves finished second in their group behind Yugoslavia.

In the lead-up to the match, Craig Brown fought hard to have the fixture moved from Hibernian's Easter Road stadium in Edinburgh to Celtic Park. Brown felt strongly about this matter, understandably craving an attendance of 50,000 in Glasgow to roar his team towards France 98 rather than the 16,500 who would be able to cram into Easter Road. After much deliberation with the SFA and Hibernian FC, common sense eventually prevailed, and the venue for this crucial match was switched.

The Latvia match took place on Saturday 11 October 1997. With Colin Hendry fit again, the most noteworthy change in Scotland's line-up saw Christian Dailly retain his place, but at the expense of Tosh McKinlay at left wing-back. McKinlay had performed impressively during the campaign, and could have considered himself unlucky to lose his place to Dailly. The other change from the Belarus match at Pittodrie saw Gordon Durie replace Darren Jackson, who was not able to join the squad due to illness. In front of a full house, Scotland made no mistake, scoring at the perfect moment just before half time to ease the nerves after dominating the ball for 42 minutes with no reward. Gallacher scored the goal once again, his sixth of the campaign, after Collins had struck an accurate shot with his left foot from outside the area that Latvian goalkeeper Olegs Karavajevs could only parry. The ball bounced free in the box and Gallacher reacted first, a typical feature of his play, to cushion a lovely header into the empty net. The Scotland players mobbed Collins and Gallacher ecstatically, as France 98 now beckoned.

On 72 minutes, Durie rounded off one of the Tartan Army's most memorable days, after a terrific run and cross from the right wing by Craig Burley caused chaos in the Latvian penalty area. The irrepressible Gallacher latched onto the ball and chipped the goalkeeper, who watched the ball sail over his head and bounce back off the crossbar. Rather like the first goal, Durie was free to cushion the rebound with a header from close range into the unguarded goal. The Scotland players performed a lap of honour for the rapturous Tartan Army. Now Craig Brown would turn his attention to securing a suitable squad camp for the World Cup finals.

4

THE SQUAD

Six months prior to the naming of his squad, Craig Brown had travelled to the FIFA World Cup draw, held on Thursday 4 December 1997 at the Stade Vélodrome, Marseille. At the draw, Brown had swapped pleasantries with the managers of the other successful qualifying European nations, among them England's Glenn Hoddle, Germany's Berti Vogts, the Netherlands' Guus Hiddink, France's Aimé Jacquet and Denmark's Bo Johansson. A Europe versus the Rest of the World exhibition match preceded the marquee event, with Brown expected to provide a Scottish player to feature. Injury prevented Brown's first choice of Gary McAllister travelling to participate, and Gordon Durie played in the match instead, appearing as a second-half substitute for Scotland's Euro 96 nemesis, the Netherlands' Patrick Kluivert. The match finished in a 5–2 victory for the Rest of the World, with Brazilian superstar Ronaldo and Argentinian goal machine Gabriel Batistuta each netting two goals before half-time. Romania's Marius Lacatus had put Europe ahead before Colombia's Antony de Avila, assisted by Ronaldo, had brought parity, before the Rest of the World ran riot. As a foretaste of France 98 to come, French superstar Zinedine Zidane pulled back another goal for the Europeans in the second half when he rounded Paraguayan goalkeeper Rubén Ruiz Díaz and lashed home from a tight angle.

While in France, the meticulous Brown also took the opportunity to travel to St-Rémy-de-Provence for a second time, to meet the mayor of the commune, and to confirm a hotel complex as Scotland's France 98 base. As for the draw itself, Brown must have had a premonition, as he had repeated in press conferences beforehand that his greatest wish was to avoid Brazil at the group stage. Brown assessed that drawing Brazil would almost certainly mean that the other nations in their group would be competing for second place. Inevitably, Scotland were then drawn in Group A alongside Brazil, as well as Norway and Morocco. In a quirk of fate, the draw meant Scotland would now face Brazil, as holders, on 10 June 1998, in the opening match of France 98, creating undoubtedly the biggest fixture in the history of the Scotland National Team. Having settled on the St Rémy base, and learned who he would be facing at France 98, Brown now turned his attention to forming a 22-man squad.

Scotland's early preparations in 1998 comprised friendly matches against Denmark at Ibrox in March and Finland at Easter Road in April. Prior to this, Scotland's final match of 1997 had taken place in Saint-Etienne against France on 12 November. France, as tournament hosts, did not need to qualify, and were seeking opponents for friendly matches. Brown later described leading a team discussion before the match, during which he asked Scotland's players to identify France's leader on the pitch. Brown states that several names were touted, including Didier Deschamps, Marcel Desailly and Patrick Vieira.

Nobody, however, mentioned France's number ten, Zinedine Zidane, who despite the flash of brilliance shown in that World Cup draw showpiece in Marseille in December 1997 had not yet been catapulted to the status of global football superstar and national hero. This, of course, would occur seven months later at the conclusion of France 98.

In terms of squad inclusions, Brown fielded three players in Saint-Etienne who had not featured in any of the qualification matches: defenders David Weir of Hearts and debutant Matt Elliott of Leicester City, and goalkeeper Neil Sullivan of Wimbledon. Scotland were beaten 2-1 on the day by a French team close to full strength, with France's goals scored by Pierre Laigle and Youri Djorkaeff, either side of Scotland's reply, which Gordon Durie netted. The countdown for France 98 had now begun in earnest, and overall Brown deemed this a credible performance against formidable opponents, providing him with much cause for optimism.

By the time Scotland's next match came around against Denmark on 25 March 1998, the World Cup draw had taken place, and the fierce competition for squad positions was now in full swing. In an evening kick-off at Ibrox, Brown's team was as follows:

> Jim Leighton (sub Andy Goram, 46 mins), Jackie McNamara (sub David Weir, 59 mins), Tom Boyd, Colin Hendry (captain), Matt Elliott, Colin Calderwood, Christian Dailly, Scot Gemmill (sub

Stuart McCall, 70 mins), Billy McKinlay, Darren Jackson (sub Simon Donnelly, 76 mins), Scott Booth (sub Eoin Jess, 46 mins).

In a line-up that appeared to include four centre-backs in Hendry, Elliott, Dailly and Calderwood, Brown deployed Calderwood as a defensive midfielder to man-mark the wonderfully talented Michael Laudrup. Michael's brother Brian, then of Rangers, another outstanding footballer, was also playing for Denmark on the night, and scored the only goal of the game on 38 minutes with a thumping right-footed strike. This goal arguably came against the run of play, and despite Scotland's line-up appearing to be ultra-defensive on paper, Brown's progressive and high-pressing 3–5–2 formation continued to look fluent and cohesive.

The hardworking Jackson, something of an unsung hero for Scotland, continued to be highly effective in international football, as he floated from advanced positions into the midfield to steal the ball and keep up the momentum in Scotland's play. Applying modern football terminology, Jackson's role in the side might now be considered leading a 'high press'. Boyd was another indispensable player, equally comfortable playing at centre-back or wing-back. Dailly had also recently emerged in the same mould as Boyd positionally, and Craig Brown now increasingly favoured his versatility. Dailly was by no means an unknown quantity either, and to date is Scotland's most capped player at Under-21 level, making 35 appearances between 1990 and 1996. Dailly, initially a forward with Dundee United, converted to defence with considerable success, first earning a move to the English Premier League with Derby County before signing for Blackburn Rovers for over £5 million.

The Danes, on the other hand, had mostly played a long-ball game until they scored, but in the Laudrup brothers possessed two players of genuine world-class quality who could change a game in a moment. Equally, despite being on top for much of the first half, Scotland had lacked the quality in the final third possessed by Denmark, who dominated the match after taking the lead.

In what was another useful exercise for Craig Brown, he was forced to consider other squad options after losing a number of key players to injury in the lead-up to the Denmark fixture. The six players were captain Gary McAllister, Paul Lambert, John Collins, Craig Burley, Kevin Gallacher and Gordon Durie. This gave Billy McKinlay and Scot Gemmill the chance to deputise in midfield. On the night, Gemmill did his squad chances no harm with an industrious performance, and McKinlay in particular took his opportunity to stake his claim with a commanding midfield performance. In attack, Booth worked hard for little reward, but in doing so demonstrated he fitted with Brown's expectations of his forwards within the 3–5–2 system. Booth, on loan at Utrecht from Borussia Dortmund at the time, did not look like he would supplant qualification hero Gallacher from the starting eleven, but nonetheless provided capable cover, and had major tournament experience with two appearances at Euro 96 already under his belt. In defence, Elliott of Leicester City made his first appearance as a starter, and also proved himself as solid defensive squad cover. Goram's appearance as a half-time substitute for Leighton in goal for Scotland would be his 43rd and final cap, the context of which is detailed extensively in the following chapter.

The second half against Denmark also saw the introduction of the talented but enigmatic Jess of Aberdeen as a substitute for his old clubmate and strike partner Booth. Jess had been part of Brown's Euro 96 squad, but did not play in France 98 qualification. At one stage Jess had been a likely starter for Brown against Latvia and Estonia away, but withdrew from the squad for personal reasons following the death of his father. Twice the Scottish PFA Young Player of the Year in his first spell with Aberdeen, Jess had now returned to the Dons after a difficult spell in the English Premier League with Coventry City after a big-money move. Jess showed glimpses of his talent after coming off the bench, but was unavailable for the next match against Finland due to sciatica, and ultimately did not make Brown's final 22-man squad.

Fortunately, key men Lambert, Collins, Gallacher and Durie would return to the squad for the Finland match, which took place on 22 April 1998 at Easter Road. Burley, however, temporarily remained on the casualty list. The big injury news was that Gary McAllister would now definitely miss France 98 after another setback. McAllister had damaged his cruciate ligament in December 1997 and had had knee surgery, but had remained hopeful he could return to action and match fitness in time to captain Scotland at France 98. However, in early March 1998, McAllister's knee gave way once again in his comeback match, a reserve fixture for his club Coventry City, and he now faced a further eight months on the sidelines. This was a harsh blow for the talented McAllister, who had travelled to the 1990 World Cup in Italy under Andy Roxburgh, but had remained an unused substitute. McAllister would now conclude his international career as Scotland's joint-record appearance maker at the European Championships, but unfortunately without an appearance at a World Cup finals.

In McAllister's absence, Colin Hendry had captained

Scotland against Denmark, and would retain the captain's armband for the forthcoming Finland match. The Scotland line-up for the fixture was as follows:

Jim Leighton, Christian Dailly (sub Tom Boyd, 85 mins), Colin Calderwood (sub Gordon Durie, 70 mins), Colin Hendry (captain), Matt Elliott (sub David Weir, 46 mins), Derek Whyte, John Collins, Scot Gemmill (sub Paul Lambert, 75 mins), Billy McKinlay, Darren Jackson (sub Kevin Gallacher, 46 mins), Scott Booth (sub Simon Donnelly, 75 mins).

As usual, Brown deployed his 3–5–2 formation, with Whyte coming in at left centre-back, and Elliott holding his place at right centre-back, either side of captain Hendry in central defence. Whyte, a highly-rated youngster while at Celtic who had spent five seasons in England at Middlesbrough and had latterly returned to Scottish football at Aberdeen, had won his first cap over ten years earlier in the unsuccessful Euro 88 qualifying campaign. Whyte had also been an unused substitute at the Euro 92 and Euro 96 finals, and was winning his 11th cap of a 12-cap international career. On the night, Dailly would shift from left centre-back to left wing-back, and Calderwood unusually assumed the right wing-back position. Calderwood, increasingly viewed as a utility player for club Tottenham Hotspur, had developed an excellent understanding with Hendry in Scotland's defence during qualification, and would be an expected starter in the right centre-back position at France 98. In midfield and attack, Gemmill, Billy McKinlay, Jackson and Booth retained their places from the Denmark match, with

Collins reintroduced to the starting line-up. Leighton was retained as goalkeeper, with Goram ruled out with a hamstring injury.

After Celtic Park had been preferred for the final home qualifier the previous year, the Finland match was the first Scotland international to be played in Edinburgh for 60 years, and a full house at Easter Road provided a good atmosphere in what was to be Scotland's last match before Brown was scheduled to name his final squad the following month. For those interested in the history of the kits worn by the Scotland National Team, this match was Scotland's first match in their new Umbro home kit, later worn at France 98.

The match itself was competitive, with the Finns providing awkward opposition, and Brown describing his team on the night as 'experimental'. Brown was nonetheless criticised in the Scottish press after Scotland could only manage a 1–1 draw on the night.

Finland had taken the lead on ten minutes after Scotland's unfamiliar defence did not deal with a long, hopeful ball that allowed Jonatan Johansson of Rangers to run in behind and calmly slot the ball past Leighton. Scotland's Elliott appeared to misjudge the flight of the ball slightly, which was rough justice on a player who had otherwise played extremely well in his first two international starts. Undoubtedly a physical presence, Elliott had also shown himself to be comfortable on the ball with a good range of passing.

Scotland's reply came only five minutes later when Jackson controlled the ball and tapped in from close range at the far post after Antti Niemi, also of Rangers, saved a Dailly header in the Finland goal.

The friendlies against Denmark and Finland were both

played in a competitive spirit, and had provided Brown with a valuable final opportunity to run the rule over his squad options. Brown was scheduled to name his 22-man squad ahead of a trip to the USA to acclimatise and play two final friendlies, against Colombia in New York and the USA in Washington DC. Prior to naming this squad, Brown confirmed the 22-man squad for the USA trip would constitute his final France 98 squad, and changes would only now arise due to injuries or withdrawals incurred in the USA.

Craig Brown named his final France 98 squad on 13 May 1998 as follows:

Goalkeepers: Jim Leighton (Aberdeen), Andy Goram (Rangers) (withdrew), Neil Sullivan (Wimbledon), Jonathan Gould (Celtic) (replacement).

Defenders: Tom Boyd (Celtic), Christian Dailly (Derby County), Matt Elliott (Leicester City), Colin Hendry (Blackburn Rovers), Tosh McKinlay (Celtic), David Weir (Hearts), Derek Whyte (Aberdeen), Colin Calderwood (Tottenham Hotspur), Jackie McNamara (Celtic).

Midfielders: Craig Burley (Celtic), John Collins (Monaco), Scot Gemmill (Nottingham Forest), Paul Lambert (Celtic), Billy McKinlay (Blackburn Rovers).

Forwards: Scott Booth (Utrecht, on loan from Borussia Dortmund), Simon Donnelly (Celtic), Gordon Durie (Rangers), Darren Jackson (Celtic), Kevin Gallacher (Blackburn Rovers).

Of the 29 players who had played for Scotland in France 98 qualification, the following eleven players were not part of Craig Brown's 22-man squad: Duncan Ferguson, Stuart McCall, Ally McCoist, Gary McAllister, John Spencer, Billy Dodds, John McGinlay, Paul McStay, Ian Ferguson, David Hopkin and Brian McAllister.

As detailed in the next chapter, Goram withdrew during the USA trip in contentious circumstances, to be replaced by uncapped Gould, who had kept 24 clean sheets in 48 appearances for Celtic during the 1997–98 season. Gould, whose father Bobby was manager of the Wales National Team at the time, was a charismatic squad addition at the eleventh hour, and the only squad change made to Brown's original 22. After Goram's shock departure, Sullivan, who had won two caps, was promoted to second-choice goalkeeper behind Leighton, who would now certainly start in France.

There had been no great surprises in relation to Brown's final defensive choices, with Dailly, Elliott and Weir playing themselves into Brown's thoughts and plans in the preceding months. Dailly, by now a mainstay in Scotland's first eleven, had not featured until the eighth qualification match, while Elliott and Weir had not played in qualification at all. After a solid performance against Finland, Whyte would now travel to his third major tournament as defensive cover, and despite having fallen down the pecking order slightly in recent months, Tosh McKinlay had justifiably made the final cut after some excellent earlier performances in qualification. The only defender who featured in qualification and missed out was Brian McAllister, who had come on as a late substitute against Belarus away from home.

Scotland's first defensive choices for France 98 would remain Hendry, Calderwood and Boyd, with Hendry in particular now a colossus at international level. Hendry's club credentials were no less impressive, with an English Premier League winner's medal to his name, won with Blackburn Rovers in 1994–95. It was anticipated that Dailly's versatility would also secure him game time in France. Most recently, Dailly had performed well at left wing-back against Finland, a position that combined Dailly's previous experience as a forward with his more recent incarnation as a defender. Dailly could also be switched in-game to centre-back, which was likely to give him the edge over other defensive hopefuls. McNamara, Scottish PFA Player of the Year for the 1997–98 season, was in contention for the right wing-back position.

There were no great revelations in Brown's midfield choices either, with Lambert and Collins both having gained a wealth of top-level experience at club level, and both expected to start in France. Collins, who could speak French, had reached the Champions League semi-finals with Monaco during this season, and Lambert had his Champions League winner's medal from the previous season with Borussia Dortmund. Burley was in contention for both central midfield and the right wing-back position. Burley had won the Scottish Football Writers' Association (SFWA) Player of the Year award in 1997–98 playing in central midfield, and was known to favour this role over the right wing-back position. Gemmill and Billy McKinlay had both played competently against Denmark and Finland, and were in the frame for game time in France.

Several midfielders who played in qualification missed the France 98 squad. Gary McAllister, as mentioned above, missed out through injury. Stuart McCall's omission is covered in greater detail in the following chapter. Paul McStay, fifth on Scotland's all-time record appearance list with 76 caps, won his final four caps during qualification. In an international career which began in 1983, McStay played in three major tournaments for Scotland: World Cups Mexico 86 and Italia 1990, and Euro 92 in Sweden. The other two midfielders who played in qualification and did not travel were Ian Ferguson and David Hopkin. Ferguson, a combative midfielder, is one of the most decorated Scottish footballers of all time, having won all of Rangers' nine league titles in a row between 1989 and 1997. Ferguson also won the Scottish Cup on four occasions, including with St Mirren in 1987 alongside Paul Lambert, and won the Scottish League Championship for the tenth time with Rangers in the 1998–99 season. Despite an incredible list of domestic honours, Ferguson played only nine times for Scotland in an international career that began in 1989. The cap Ferguson won during qualification in the rescheduled match against Estonia in Monaco was his ninth and final appearance. While Ferguson, like McStay, was coming to the end of a long successful career, Hopkin, on the other hand, was 28 years old, and later said he was extremely disappointed to be left out. This is understandable, as Hopkin was playing for Leeds United in the English Premier League and had scored two well-taken goals in qualification against Belarus.

Overall, it was Craig Brown's choice of forwards that created the most controversy. The omission of Ally McCoist, covered in detail in the next chapter, had left the squad without an orthodox striker. Of those forwards who were included, Gallacher had been the most prolific during qualification, scoring six crucial goals. The experienced Gallacher was now travelling to his third major tournament, having played at Euro 92 and Euro 96, and was also in good scoring form in the English Premier League with his club

Blackburn Rovers. Alongside Gallacher, the experienced Durie was now travelling to his fourth major tournament, having played at the World Cup in 1990, Euro 92 and Euro 96. Jackson was Brown's third forward of choice, a squad place that was undoubtedly merited after his outstanding contribution in several crucial qualifiers. The statistic of concern, however, was that Gallacher had a total of eight international goals, Durie had a total of seven and Jackson had a total of four. This totalled 19 international goals between Scotland's three main forwards, while McCoist had scored 19 international goals on his own!

Booth, the forward chosen over McCoist, had scored five international goals, but had not found the net for Scotland since Euro 96 qualification, and had not played in the France 98 qualifiers. Brown's final chosen forward was Simon Donnelly of Celtic, who at 23 years old was the youngest member of the squad. Donnelly had won a total of eight caps, mostly as a late substitute, with no goals scored. Donnelly had been a hero of Celtic's recent title win, scoring a respectable ten league goals in 30 appearances during the season, and Brown evidently saw Donnelly as the future of Scotland's forward line.

Of the forwards other than McCoist who played in qualification and did not travel to France 98, Duncan Ferguson, as detailed in the previous chapter, had retired early from international football. John McGinlay of Bolton Wanderers and latterly Bradford City, who had scored the vital winner against Sweden during qualification, had now suffered a serious Achilles tendon injury that required surgery, effectively ending his playing career. John Spencer, who had started the match against England at Wembley in Euro 96, had now dropped a division in English football, having been sold to Queens Park Rangers by Chelsea. Spencer had played just one match during qualification, against Latvia in 1996, and had since dropped out of international contention. Conversely, the international career of Billy Dodds of Aberdeen, who had featured three times as a substitute during qualification but missed the 22-man cut for France 98, gained more traction in the Euro 2000 qualification campaign that followed.

The first step for Scotland's 22-man squad was a flight to New Jersey on 19 May 1998 for a training camp and to play friendly matches against Colombia and the USA. These USA trips were by now a tried-and-trusted preparatory process for the Scotland National Team on the eve of a major tournament. Indeed, Scotland had played friendly matches against the same two nations in the USA just prior to Euro 96, where the squad had been put through their paces in high temperatures during an intense fortnight of training. It was during this previous USA trip in May 1996 that Rod Stewart had made contact with the Scottish delegation to say that he was playing a concert in Madison Square Garden and intended to come and watch Scotland versus the USA in Connecticut. Craig Brown recalls Rod Stewart inviting the Scottish World Cup squad of 1986 to his home in Los Angeles, and Brown felt it was now time to return the favour. Much to the delight of the press, Stewart was then invited to join Scotland for training, which he accepted. Much to the disgust of the Rangers players, Stewart turned up to train wearing a Celtic tracksuit and kit, and was quickly provided with replacement Scotland training apparel. Afterwards, Stewart provided 32 tickets for the Madison Square Garden gig, and Brown

The Squad

and his squad were invited on stage on their arrival in the arena.

Aside from providing occasional unforgettable memories for the squad like appearing on stage with rock 'n' roll legends, these training camps largely comprised punishing training sessions in searing temperatures. As we will discover in the following chapter, Andy Goram would latterly become one of Craig Brown's fiercest critics, but he praised Brown for the intensity of the 1996 USA trip, assessing that the peak level of squad fitness obtained in the camp was the primary reason for Scotland's impressive draw against the Netherlands in the first match of Euro 96. Though Goram's shock withdrawal from the France 98 USA camp, which I will detail shortly, overshadowed the New York leg of the trip, the players were nevertheless satisfied with the comfortable hotel facilities on arrival in Short Hills, New Jersey, as they prepared to face Colombia in New York's Giants Stadium. The Scotland line-up for the Colombia fixture on 23 May 1998 was as follows:

Neil Sullivan, Christian Dailly, Tom Boyd (sub Jackie McNamara, 71 mins), Colin Calderwood, Colin Hendry (captain), Craig Burley, John Collins, Paul Lambert, Billy McKinlay, Darren Jackson (sub Scott Booth, 46 mins), Gordon Durie (sub Simon Donnelly, 61 mins).

The match itself was another useful friendly played in a competitive spirit, which finished in a 2–2 draw. Scotland had fallen behind to a soft penalty conceded by Dailly, which was dispatched by the flamboyant Colombian captain Carlos Valderrama. Scotland then equalised through a fine right-footed strike from John Collins after he was teed up neatly by Darren Jackson. A collector's piece, given that a goal of this quality might have been expected from Collins' left foot, as opposed to his weaker right. Nine minutes later, Scotland then took the lead through Craig Burley, who was released on the left flank by another excellent pass from Jackson, and slammed the ball home from a difficult angle. Afterwards, Brown and the players considered this a good Scotland performance but one that perhaps deserved a win.

Thankfully for Craig Brown, Goram's departure was the only significant drama in New York. However, there was another near miss on this leg of the trip that would have made the tabloids had it been known at the time, the story of which Paul Lambert later recounted in *A Bhoy's Own Story*. One evening, the squad had a night out in the Big Apple, with strict instructions to be back on board their coach departing the city centre by 1am. Colin Hendry, Paul Lambert, John Collins, Jim Leighton, Colin Calderwood, Kevin Gallacher and Tom Boyd went for a meal and a few drinks, but lost track of the time and distance back to the pick-up point. Unbelievably, this led to six of Scotland's key squad members for an imminent World Cup running through the middle of New York at 1am and taking a shortcut through a fish market, where they slipped and slid across the drenched market floor as they dashed for the coach. To add insult to their near miss with injury, they arrived a minute or two late at their rendezvous point, and the coach had departed without them. This then led to a nightmare with New York City's taxis, as two cabs were required, and one driver did not know how to get to Short Hills. By this time, the players involved, preparing for one of the biggest matches in world football against Brazil, were understandably losing their cool. The problem was ultimately resolved by hiring a limousine from a hotel, which got them back to their own hotel at 3am. Alex Miller was on guard duty on their arrival back at Short Hills, and the players covered their embarrassment by blaming the prompt departure of the coach. Now it's just an amusing anecdote, but can you imagine the headlines and regret if an avoidable accident in a fish market had cost Scotland their captain, goalkeeper or other key member of the first eleven for France 98!?

After New York, the squad then travelled to Washington to prepare for their final friendly match before the World Cup finals. While in Washington, Scotland were based in Tyson's Corner, where the players were reportedly less satisfied with the facilities. This was partly because the hotel was too far from the city to allow the players to experience the American capital, though at least it lessened the chances of late-night injuries sustained by taking shortcuts. The Scotland line-up for the USA fixture on 30 May 1998 was as follows:

Jim Leighton, Christian Dailly, Tom Boyd, Colin Calderwood, Colin Hendry (captain), Tosh McKinlay (sub Jackie McNamara, 59 mins), John Collins, Paul Lambert, Billy McKinlay (sub Craig Burley, 74 mins), Darren Jackson, Kevin Gallacher (sub Simon Donnelly, 82 mins).

Scotland's match against the USA at Robert F Kennedy Memorial Stadium was best remembered for the incredible temperatures on the day, which pushed the mercury into the high-30s Celsius and impacted the game as a spectacle. In fact, afterwards some Scotland players expressed a level of discontent at being asked to play in the baking heat, which they felt had verged on dangerous. Over 46,000 attended a 0–0 draw, with Scotland's best chance falling to Kevin Gallacher, who had found himself one versus one with USA goalkeeper Kasey Keller, after yet another fine lobbed pass from Darren Jackson. With plenty of time and space to choose his spot, Gallacher shot straight at Keller, who saved well. The best chance for the USA fell to Roy Wegerle, who hit the bar from close range.

Craig Brown's France 98 preparations were now almost complete, and after the match the squad flew straight home to Scotland, where the buzz was steadily growing, as the World Cup finals beckoned. However, the story of Brown's high-profile squad omissions still had plenty left to run, and that is the subject of the next chapter.

5
SMELL THE GLOVE

The naming of a 22-man squad for a major international tournament inevitably causes controversy and can lead to disagreements that last decades. Craig Brown's naming of his France 98 Scotland squad was no exception. Throw in the age-old rivalry between Scotland's top two clubs from the Old Firm and the politics of club football spilling into the National Team set-up and there is always the potential for fireworks.

Brown had fielded 29 players in Scotland's ten France 98 qualification matches as follows: Andy Goram, Craig Burley, Tom Boyd, Colin Calderwood, Colin Hendry, Tosh McKinlay, Duncan Ferguson, Stuart McCall, Ally McCoist, Gary McAllister, John Collins, Gordon Durie, Derek Whyte, John Spencer, Darren Jackson, Paul Lambert, Billy Dodds (of Aberdeen), Jackie McNamara, Jim Leighton (by now back at Aberdeen), Billy McKinlay, John McGinlay, Kevin Gallacher, Paul McStay, Ian Ferguson (Rangers), Scot Gemmill, Christian Dailly, David Hopkin, Brian McAllister (Wimbledon) and Simon Donnelly (Celtic). Following the World Cup draw, competition for squad places had never been fiercer, and the dramatic conclusion of the 1997–98 Scottish league season adds significant context to the controversy that was to follow Brown's squad selection. The domestic season had ended with an unexpected league title for Celtic under short-lived manager Wim Jansen, twice a World Cup finalist as a player for the Netherlands. At the conclusion of the previous season, Rangers had clinched their ninth consecutive Scottish League Championship, thus matching the remarkable achievement of Jock Stein's Celtic between 1966 and 1974. In a run that began under Graeme Souness in 1989, Rangers had thereafter swept aside all that lay before them over nine memorable seasons for the club. Within the bubble of the perpetual oneupmanship culture of the Old Firm, Rangers had dreamed of ten league titles in a row. However, Celtic under Jansen had clinched the league title on the last day of the season after a dramatic run-in, and Rangers had then gone on to lose the Scottish Cup Final against Hearts.

To rub salt in the wounds, manager Walter Smith, at the helm for six full seasons of Rangers' nine-in-a-row success, had stated his intention to step down at the end of the season. Smith would be replaced by the authoritarian Dutchman Dick Advocaat, who had immediately made it clear he did not wish to retain some of the big names and big characters of Rangers' nine-in-a-row squad. Three players who were now surplus to requirements at Ibrox were Scotland internationals Ally McCoist, Andy Goram and Stuart McCall. McCoist, now aged 35, was Rangers' all-time record goalscorer with an incredible 355 goals in 581 appearances. McCall, aged 33, was a tenacious midfielder with as much major tournament experience as any other outfield player available. Goram, aged 34, was revered by fans and fellow professionals alike. Indeed, the respect for Goram's goalkeeping prowess had crossed the Old Firm divide, with Goram's friend and ex-Celtic manager Tommy Burns famously once stating, 'Put it on my tombstone... Andy Goram broke my heart.' Paul Lambert, a title winner for Celtic under Jansen in 1997–98, also compared a save made by Goram for Scotland against Estonia during France 98 qualification to Gordon Banks' famous save for England from a Pelé header for Brazil at the 1970 World Cup in Mexico.

Brown named his 22-man squad on 13 May 1998, just ahead of the Scottish Cup Final between Rangers and Hearts on 16 May, and it was the omission of Ally McCoist that created the most controversy. McCoist was massively popular, and although nearing the end of his career, it was widely felt he still had a goal or two in him at the very highest level. This was proven when McCoist netted a consolation goal for Rangers in the 81st minute of the Scottish Cup Final itself, in what was his final game before leaving to conclude his club career with Kilmarnock. McCoist scored 16 goals in 26 appearances for Rangers during the 1997–98 season, and had been in fine form in the latter part of the season. McCoist was also vastly experienced at international level, having won 59 caps and scored 19 goals, including a winner against Switzerland at Euro 96 only two years earlier. McCoist's trophy-laden Rangers career had ended on a negative note, and when he learned he was not included in Brown's France 98 squad, he was heartbroken, later citing his omission as his all-time career low.

To this day, Brown's omission of McCoist remains

baffling, and on this subject Brown has given up ground as the years have gone by. In an interview with BBC Sport in May 2018, Brown stated that he looked back on his decision to omit McCoist 'with great regret', having felt compelled to publicly apologise to McCoist at a speaking engagement two weeks earlier for what he now considers a mistake. Ironically, Brown also devotes several pages to stories and anecdotes involving McCoist in *Craig Brown: The Autobiography*, published just a week after Brown announced the France 98 squad, while simultaneously describing how he brought about the most traumatic experience in the striker's career. When initially describing his rationale for this decision, prior to his later concessions that he made a mistake, Brown simplified the matter to a great extent. Despite McCoist having declared himself fit to play, which was proven in the Scottish Cup Final, Brown stated at the time that he was worried about a calf injury McCoist had been carrying. Brown then travelled to watch striker Scott Booth play for Utrecht in the Dutch league on the eve of France 98, and decided to include him over McCoist. Booth had not played in France 98 qualification, and later played only seven minutes of the tournament itself.

Andy Goram had starred at Euro 96 in England, but had played in only three of the ten France 98 qualification matches after sustaining a serious thigh injury in March 1997. The void created by Goram's absence had led to the resurgence of veteran goalkeeper Jim Leighton, who turned in some excellent performances in the final five qualification matches. Goram, opposite in personality to the reserved Leighton, had often been the subject of tabloid headlines due to relationship problems and a hard-drinking lifestyle. In the summer of 1998, Goram was despondent due to his

Rangers career ending on a low, but had nonetheless regained match fitness, and was still widely considered Scotland's best goalkeeper. Goram, the younger man by five years, also considered himself Scotland's rightful number one for France 98.

Goram's international career had begun in 1985 at the age of 21 in Alex Ferguson's first match as Scotland manager, and he had been an unused World Cup substitute at both Mexico 86 and Italia 90, where Leighton had played in all three matches of both tournaments. At the World Cup in 1990, Leighton had only recently emerged from the most traumatic moment of his career, after being dropped by Alex Ferguson for the replay of the 1990 FA Cup Final when playing for Manchester United. Goram felt he should have played at the 1990 World Cup due to Leighton's crisis in confidence, but Andy Roxburgh had stuck by Leighton for the tournament.

After 43 caps and a decorated domestic career, Goram therefore felt he had earned the right to play at the World Cup. As manager of Scotland's Under-21s, Brown had also picked Goram for teams dating back to 1986, and at Euro 96 he had witnessed Goram in the form of his life at a major tournament. Goram had also played in all three matches of Euro 92, and to date jointly shares Scotland's appearances record at the European Championships alongside Gary McAllister and Stuart McCall on six appearances. Brown therefore knew that Goram had the temperament, talent and experience to handle the big occasion.

As we have seen, Scotland's schedule in the lead-up to France 98 began with friendly matches against Denmark in March and Finland in April 1998. Following these friendlies, Brown then selected 22 players for a pre-World Cup trip to the USA in May, and theoretically the same 22 players were set to become Brown's final squad for France 98. Goram was named in the squad of 22 and travelled to the USA, but during the trip learned from a non-playing SFA staff member that Brown would be naming Leighton as his starting goalkeeper at France 98. These events occurred a mere three weeks before the tournament, timing that Goram felt was completely unacceptable for a player of his stature. What happened next was explosive, and Brown's handling of Goram in many ways typifies his tenure as Scotland manager. Goram decided there and then that he was leaving the USA training camp and retiring from international football.

In his brutally honest autobiography, *The Goalie*, Goram accuses Brown of hiding from the big decisions, and calls Brown a diplomat who was too intent on keeping everyone happy. He claims Brown's man-management was poor, and draws the comparison with Euro 96, where the goalkeepers were told who would be playing at the tournament similarly late in the day. At Euro 96, Leighton had been the unlucky recipient of Brown's bad news and had been left heartbroken. Goram is also highly critical of Brown's response to his decision to leave the USA camp. As Scotland's France 98 story developed, Brown became increasingly media-conscious, and Goram claims Brown came to his hotel room prior to his departure merely to ask him not to fly into Glasgow Airport, where he knew the Scottish press would be waiting.

In *The Goalie*, Goram describes his relationship with Brown as tense and uncomfortable, and recollects an earlier clash with Brown in the Ibrox home dressing room when on international duty. This followed Brown insisting that the dressing room was too big and telling Goram to move from his usual longstanding dressing room peg to allow Brown to cut the dressing room in half. Goram recollects feeling superstitious about the peg, and telling Brown he had won all his medals from the seat and would not be moving, leading to a heated dressing-room stand-off. Goram is also highly critical of the value placed by Brown on matters that he viewed as trivial, for example, Brown's insistence that all players must look the same at all times, so if one player wore tracksuit bottoms at training, all players must wear them. Brown also insisted that shirts must be tucked in when playing, and that sock tape must match sock colour. Goram viewed these rules as 'laughable' and 'pathetic', and felt Brown was treating him 'like a schoolkid in one of his classrooms'. Similar criticism was also levelled at Brown's predecessor Andy Roxburgh, even by his close ally Jim Leighton in his own autobiography, *In the Firing Line*, and was a pitfall that Brown was consciously trying to avoid.

Eight years earlier, Roxburgh had stood by his number one, Leighton, at Italia 90, but Brown had now arguably chosen to abandon his de facto number one during his hour of need. In Goram's view, Brown had robbed him of his deserved chance to play at the World Cup. Goram describes being plagued by regret over this experience and feels Brown cheated him of the piece of the jigsaw that would have completed an exceptional career. Goram might have been flawed in some respects, but nobody can deny his honesty about his shortcomings, choices and misjudgements.

By contrast, Brown's account of the Goram incident in the USA in *The Game of My Life* is somewhat vague, which is not an isolated occurrence in Brown's recollections of the events surrounding his naming of Scotland's France 98 squad. On the day of Goram's departure, Brown describes receiving a letter from Goram as he walked to breakfast in

Scotland's New Jersey hotel base. Brown claims that he was oblivious to Goram's angst, and states that Goram cited personal problems back home in Scotland as his rationale for leaving the camp. At no stage has Brown acknowledged his alleged plan to omit Goram, the magnitude of this decision if true, or that the news was allegedly back-channelled to Goram via a third party in the USA camp. Goram's letter was arguably convenient for Brown, as it allowed him to refer to Goram's relationship difficulties as the sole reason for his shock departure, thus avoiding the confrontation his controversial decision to name Leighton ahead of Goram in the starting eleven would undoubtedly have created. Brown's account of this drama places the emphasis solely on Goram's mental state at the time, which is not a particularly endearing managerial trait in any walk of life, albeit that Brown appears merely to have cited Goram's own written words at the time.

This account is, of course, not intended to undermine or incriminate Jim Leighton, the other main protagonist in this drama. Leighton was an exceptional sportsman who had made his name at Alex Ferguson's Aberdeen, with whom Leighton had won the Scottish League Championship three times and the European Cup Winners Cup in 1982–83, famously defeating Bayern Munich in the quarter-finals and Real Madrid in the final. Leighton was also Scotland's second-most capped player, and by far the most experienced international available to Brown, having travelled to three previous World Cup tournaments, in 1982 (when he was uncapped), 1986 (capped in all three of Scotland's games) and 1990 (again, capped in all three games). After his miserable period with Manchester United, Leighton had rebuilt his career at Hibs in the mid-1990s and performed brilliantly during France 98 qualification.

Interestingly, in *In the Firing Line*, Leighton claims that Goram's source in the Scotland camp who had passed on the news of his forthcoming omission was Alan Hodgkinson, Scotland's vastly experienced goalkeeping coach. Hodgkinson, a former England international goalkeeper, had been Goram's mentor since his early career at Oldham Athletic and during his glory days at Rangers. Leighton had also been coached by Hodgkinson at Manchester United, but describes a falling out with Hodgkinson over coaching methods with Scotland, which Leighton felt were tailored to Goram's needs. Leighton describes his fallout with Hodgkinson as so severe that he confronted Brown's number two Alex Miller in the USA over the matter, just prior to Goram's dramatic walkout. Leighton also claims that Hodgkinson falsely told Brown that he did not wish to play in Scotland's friendly international versus France just prior to the World Cup draw in November 1997, costing him his place in the starting line-up at the expense of Neil Sullivan. Leighton's rift with Hodgkinson ultimately led to his international retirement shortly after France 98, denying him the accolade of becoming only the second player to reach 100 international caps for Scotland.

In Scotland's perpetual goalkeeping soap opera, Goram also then launched his own backlash against a key member of Brown's France 98 backroom staff. In *The Goalie*, Goram claims masseur Stewart MacMillan, a part of Brown's inner circle, created the famous 'Smell the Glove' tabloid headlines at his expense in 1997–98. Goram alleges that MacMillan inexplicably provided the *News of the World* with a false story, stating that he had thrown a goalkeeper glove into the Celtic dressing room after an Old Firm victory and shouted, 'Smell the glove,' which is an old-time boxing taunt. This, according to Goram, led to Celtic's 1997–98 title-winning team wearing T-shirts bearing the 'Smell the glove' slogan as they celebrated shattering Rangers' dreams of ten titles in a row, which left Goram feeling like a laughing stock. In *A Bhoy's Own Story*, Paul Lambert, then of Celtic, later corroborated that Goram did no such thing – he has claimed to Richard Keys and Andy Gray on beIN SPORTS as recently as 2020 that it was some random graffiti of the phrase spotted by Tosh McKinlay when Celtic were training in Kilmarnock that started it all – but the mud stuck, and Goram claims MacMillan later wrote him a letter of apology about it.

Craig Brown had undoubtedly done a tremendous job in steering Scotland to France 98, but these controversies had the potential to undermine his aim to eradicate all cliques and create a club atmosphere at international level. He had built a team which was exceptionally difficult to beat, evidenced by the loss of only three goals in qualification. Having now also successfully qualified for both Euro 96 and France 98, he was also justifiably confident in his own decisions as Scotland manager. Brown later quipped that two aircraft would have been required if he had selected every player recommended to him for his France 98 squad by the fans and media. However, having fielded only 29 players in qualification, and without an abundance of international-class players available to select from, these remarks seem exaggerated. It seems more likely that Brown was attempting to deflect debate created by his possible decision to move Goram down the pecking order and his earlier decision to omit Ally McCoist entirely. If 35-year-old McCoist was omitted in favour of 26-year-old Scott Booth, it is possible Brown was playing a long game and had assessed Scotland would travel to more major tournaments under his management.

In reality, France 98 would be the pinnacle of Brown's managerial career, and Scotland would not achieve qualification for another major tournament for the next 22 years. In the naming of his France 98 squad, Brown, dictatorial in style by his own admission, appears to have been motivated by the understandable desire to achieve total control of his France 98 camp. Some may still argue that Goram was not prepared psychologically, and McCoist was not prepared physically, but take account of Brown's further omission of the vastly experienced Stuart McCall and a decision-making pattern becomes apparent.

McCall's omission from the 22-man squad was discussed less than McCoist's, and was less dramatic than Goram's exit, but it perhaps led to the most revealing war of words. McCall's Rangers career had run in parallel with Goram's, McCall winning six of their nine league titles in a row before becoming surplus to requirements under Dick Advocaat after Walter Smith stood down as Rangers manager at the end of 1997–98. For Scotland, McCall had played at the 1990 World Cup in Italy, scoring a vital goal against Sweden. McCall was one of the most experienced international players available to Brown, and was by no means at the end of his playing career, which after leaving Rangers would span another 200 matches in the higher echelons of English football.

When discussing his France 98 disappointment in his autobiography, *The Real McCall*, McCall says that both he and McCoist were left out of the 22-man squad because Brown claimed they would 'party' in France if not included in the starting eleven. Fascinatingly, in *The Game of My Life*

Brown indeed confirms that he met Stuart McCall at a function at Parklands Leisure Centre in Newton Mearns prior to the squad announcement and that he did tell McCall that he believed McCall and McCoist would treat France 98 as a holiday if not picked. In this case, when responding to McCall's disgust, Brown positions himself in a self-created middle ground, stating that his remarks made in the leisure centre were a joke. It is difficult to imagine that McCall, omitted from a World Cup squad, would have found Brown's so-called 'joke' very funny.

Brown's various accounts of his France 98 squad selection, given in hindsight, vary from peculiarly detached to regretful in relation to his decisions. Perhaps Goram's assertion that Brown was a diplomat who wanted to be everyone's friend, and who was terrified of a bad newspaper story, is correct. Brown himself somewhat corroborates this view in *Adventures in the Golden Age*, where he says that he still tries to reckon why he left McCoist out, and that he was trying to avoid the appearance of 'an old pal's act'.

It was no secret that Rangers' nine-in-a-row team had formed a 'work hard, play hard' culture under Walter Smith and, when dissecting Brown's France 98 choices, it is possible that Brown may have sought to omit this culture completely from his final 22-man squad. Perhaps Brown took a calculated gamble when first he omitted McCoist and McCall, but did not feel he could ride out the media storm Goram's omission would create. Despite Brown's account of what occurred in New Jersey, it seems improbable that the meticulous manager was oblivious to Goram's fragile state of mind, and had not evaluated how Goram might react to the alleged leaked information provided to him secondhand prior to his shock departure. Or was this all a miscalculation by Goram's ally, coach Alan Hodgkinson? Nowhere in his later writings does Brown acknowledge that he had decided to pick Leighton prior to Goram's departure. What does seem highly likely is that this is an episode that Brown would prefer had been omitted altogether from the annals of the Scotland National Team.

6
BLATTERED

Whatever the speculation, conflicting accounts and controversy that arose from Goram's untimely exit, the USA training camp was a relative success, and on their return, the Scotland squad and SFA delegation touched down at Heathrow Airport to the waiting British media. Sensibly, Craig Brown had banned alcohol on the long-haul flight to avoid any public relations disasters, such as those experienced by the England squad on a flight back from Hong Kong on the eve of Euro 96. On arrival at Heathrow, Brown recollects he had never seen such a large media corps waiting for the Scotland National Team, and was therefore relieved his squad had abided by his alcohol ban. The squad were then granted two days off to spend with their families and instructed to meet up again on Thursday 4 June at the Westpoint Hotel, East Kilbride.

On arrival at the hotel, the first requirement of the squad was to attend a press conference. In *A Bhoy's Own Story*, Paul Lambert recollects that Scotland's media understandably had an insatiable appetite for the squad's current stories, but the players nonetheless felt the press conference was a generally positive experience. Next, the squad went for a light training session at the ground of Pollok Juniors in Glasgow before returning to the Westpoint Hotel for a kilt fitting and the official squad photograph. Captain Colin Hendry had been approached by kilt manufacturer Kinloch Anderson, who made kilts available free of charge to the entire squad for the official photograph and opening match. The players had gratefully accepted this proposition, and it would be difficult to find a better official Scotland squad photograph than the one taken at the Westpoint Hotel in national dress. Next, the squad were all measured for a set of golf clubs, which were gifted to each player by manufacturer John Letters of Scotland, another perk that pleased the players.

Orchestrated by the meticulous Brown, the squad then attended a presentation by Scottish referee Hugh Dallas, who was scheduled to referee at the tournament. Dallas provided guidance and video footage about FIFA's plans to further clamp down on tackles from behind at France 98, which was likely to lead to an increase in red cards at the finals. Dallas shared footage of recent tackles made at the top level of European football that might merit a red card rather than a yellow under the new rules, and urged the players to think twice before committing any tackles from behind.

Prophetic words indeed for the tournament ahead, and this type of planning was typical of Brown's reign, and that of Andy Roxburgh before him. With use of video footage still in its relative infancy, Roxburgh and Brown had believed in such progressive methods as part of an Aggregated Marginal Gains (AMG) approach to sports coaching. This is the theory that winning and losing at the highest level of sport can be attributed to gaining slender advantages over opponents by accumulating details that might otherwise be overlooked. Without applying the AMG approach, Roxburgh's reign as Scotland boss might have been over before it began. In 1988, Roxburgh had sent Brown to spy on a Cyprus team who were said to be masters at timewasting, and then harangued East German referee Siegfried Kirschen into playing sufficient injury time in a vital World Cup qualifier in 1989 to mitigate their opponents running down the clock. Scotland duly beat Cyprus 3–2 with a Richard Gough goal in the 96th minute. Having failed to qualify for Euro 88, a draw in Cyprus would have severely jeopardised Scotland's chances of qualifying for the 1990 World Cup, and most likely have cost Roxburgh his job. These lessons were not lost on Brown as he prepared for France 98.

On the Thursday evening of 4 June, the squad were given the option of staying at the hotel or returning home for the night, and were instructed to meet the next day at Pollok for another training session before heading to Glasgow Airport for a flight to Marseille. As the coach arrived at the airport, the sun was shining in Glasgow and a considerable crowd had gathered to see off the squad. The general mood was optimistic as Brown provided impromptu TV interviews for the Scottish news, and ad-hoc press conferences for the newspapers.

Scotland's journey to their base camp at the five-star Valrugues Hotel, St-Rémy-de-Provence, was without incident, and the squad had no difficulty settling into their comfortable surroundings. Positively, Scotland had the hotel to themselves, thanks to an SFA compensation payment to the hotel for lost revenue, which included closure of the hotel's popular restaurant to the public. Within the hotel, physiotherapist Pip Yeates had set up gym equipment, and the players had use of a games room which included pool tables, video games and a large-screen TV with comfortable seating for movies. The hotel also had a large swimming pool, and the superb training pitch where Scotland would train daily was just a short distance away in the commune of St Rémy.

These excellent facilities were in contrast with World Cups of the past, where the SFA had often booked poor facilities, lowering squad morale. The most extreme example of such a miscalculation occurred at the World Cup in Mexico in 1986, where the Scotland squad had stayed in a sparse and dingy hotel with tiny rooms, few facilities and one phone, on a street named The Avenue of the Dead! Again, Brown had experienced such SFA bungling first-hand, and it is perhaps unsurprising that he felt he must involve himself in all areas of tournament planning.

Shortly after unpacking, Scotland were expected to hold yet another press conference, this time to the world's media at the nearby St Rémy town hall. With the Brazil fixture only five days away, global media interest in the Scotland National Team was now at unprecedented levels. Craig Brown, assistant manager Alex Miller, captain Colin Hendry and France-based John Collins attended this very lively press conference. In particular, the world's media were interested in how Hendry and his Scottish defence might handle Brazilian superstar Ronaldo, the most recent winner of the Ballon d'Or, as voted for by sports writers across Europe. Hendry appeared confident in response to these questions, and the media warmed to his polite jokes and relaxed manner. Collins' ability to converse in French, in tandem with the considerable media experience of Brown and Miller, further ensured Scotland came across as far from overawed in these challenging and unique circumstances. Brown again must be given credit for his professional handling of matters during this period, and there can be little doubt that his professionalism and that of those around him was a direct result of his careful planning and strong leadership. Aside from the mildly irritating press stereotype linking the Scotland National Team to the Hollywood movie *Braveheart* – starring US-born Australian actor Mel Gibson as William Wallace, the film's eponymous hero, and still showing in Paris at the time – such press duties presented few obstacles for Brown's slick PR show.

In contrast with Scotland's professionalism, the world's press were obtaining plenty of material to fill France 98 column inches, thanks to FIFA's Executive and World Cup Organising Committees. Though the machinations within FIFA at the time only impacted the Scotland National Team as much as any of the other 31 teams at France 98, no history of the tournament is complete without a little about the backdrop to it, notably the politics and excesses of some of FIFA's now-infamous protagonists. Therefore, we briefly leave Scotland busy preparing in St Rémy and focus on what was going on some 700km north, in Paris.

In June 1998, the FIFA show was in full swing in Paris, and France 98 would be the last hurrah of one of the most controversial figures of the 20th-century, sporting or otherwise – outgoing FIFA President Dr João Havelange.

On 7 June 1998, the 51st FIFA Congress began in the Equinox Hall, Paris, where the eighth FIFA President would be named the day after, on 8 June. In the running were Havelange's pupil, FIFA's longstanding General Secretary, Sepp Blatter, and UEFA President Lennart Johansson, the Swede who had promised cultural change at FIFA since he had announced his candidacy in 1995 and a consistent sports' anti-corruption campaigner until his death in 2019.

For the occasion of France 98, Havelange had gone about his business in the usual manner, booking the £3,500-per-night presidential suite at the Bristol Hotel, Paris, along with bookings for his 80 guests. Over the six weeks he stayed in Paris, Havelange's suite alone cost £147,000, a mere formality for FIFA in 1998. Add FIFA Senior Vice-President Julio Grondona's 40 guests to this, and the 15 guests of the widow of ex-FIFA Senior Vice-President Guillermo Canedo, and you have a hotel bill of many millions. This, however, was mere chicken feed to the men who had controlled football's billions in TV and sponsorship rights for the previous 24 years.

FIFA's 51st Congress would see Sepp Blatter defeat Lennart Johansson by 111 votes to 80, thus sowing the seeds of 17 more years of similar FIFA leadership, until the FBI dismantled Blatter's FIFA administration in May 2015. To find out the full story of how Blatter achieved this and what happened in the years afterwards, I would urge you to read investigative journalist David Yallop's brilliant *How They Stole the Game*, where much of the information in this chapter is sourced.

Running parallel to the controversy around FIFA's 51st Congress and the presidential vote, France 98 had also been hitting the headlines worldwide due to an unprecedented ticket scandal. Sixty per cent of tickets were to be allocated to the French people, 20 per cent to sponsors and corporate guests, and 16 per cent to supporters, something Blatter's rival candidate Johansson had tried but failed to confirm from Blatter would happen. You will have noticed a fault with the maths – the other four per cent of France 98 tickets remain officially unaccounted for.

Michel Platini, the legendary France number ten, who was by this time also co-President of France 98, joined Blatter's presidential ticket as an obscure running mate with the promise of the job of FIFA Technical Director if Blatter became FIFA's eighth President. In the months preceding France 98, it was common knowledge that Blatter and Platini had unlimited tickets, while Johansson was frozen out with no tracking of tickets available to the World Cup Organising Committee.

The real-world impact of this chicanery on Scotland fans desperate to travel to France 98 was soon clear. When tickets went on sale in the UK, which of course included England fans as well, four million people unsuccessfully attempted to obtain tickets via a ticket phoneline in one day. Global demand exceeded supply by 5,000 to one, with only 17 authorised travel agents providing just eight per cent of tickets to normal paying football fans. Blatter explained with his trademark simplicity: 'It's just a lack of communication. There are 2.5 million tickets available – there are 25 million demands.' What was more difficult for Blatter to explain were the seemingly unlimited France 98 tickets now appearing on the black market, particularly in the USA. For the first time at the World Cup, the internet was now a factor, with American online ticket agents able to offer incredible amounts of tickets at equally incredible prices. In the documentary *FIFA Family*, French author Phillipe Auclair, author of *Fifagate*, beautifully sums up this story as '*The Sopranos*, with worse people'.

With a ticket allocation of a mere 5,000 for the opening

match of the World Cup, you can imagine the chaos these factors caused among the Tartan Army. France 98 should have been their most accessible World Cup ever. In *Adventures in the Golden Age*, Archie Macpherson recalls witnessing a 'primal hunger' for tickets, with desperate tartan-clad fans walking up and down the Champs-Elysées, crowding the pavements and begging for tickets. If you can forgive FIFA for this, you are a better person than me.

7

SIZING UP THE OPPOSITION

On 7 and 8 June 1998, Scotland's base camp at the Valrugues Hotel seemed a world away from the World Cup fever now gripping Paris and the desperate attempts by their fans to secure tickets for the Stade de France. Within their idyllic surroundings, the Scotland squad were completely removed from the drama, and therefore not witnessing the estimated 60,000 travelling Scots now pouring into the French capital. These were the days before social media, when it was possible for an international squad to disconnect completely from the outside world, and Craig Brown's preparations were running exactly as planned. In *A Bhoy's Own Story*, Paul Lambert recollects the hotel and training facilities had been met with universal approval by the squad, and the daily training sessions were attended by a decent local crowd. Lambert adds that he, John Collins, Craig Burley, Kevin Gallacher and Billy McKinlay would often return to the small stadium around five o'clock in the afternoon for an extra private session to practise free kicks. In Lambert's words, things were 'progressing nicely', and the squad were completely focused. Scotland's camp was therefore stable and organised, with all significant drama and obstacles removed by this point. Throughout France, every other qualifying nation was also setting up their tournament headquarters. This was always an exciting moment, weighing up the possibilities, likelihoods and uncertainties.

From my own personal point of view, prior to the World Cup finals, I have always been fascinated by the details emerging from each competing nation's base camp. To me, these are the facts and stories that bind the sport together, the pinnacle for worshippers of the football religion. Leaving aside Scotland's Group A for the moment, in this chapter I will therefore provide a brief overview of every competing nation at France 98. Let it act as your World Cup reference guide and transport you back to June 1998, before a ball was kicked. This will hopefully remind you of the prominent players and talking points of summer 1998 and recreate that sense of excitement as the football world descended on France for those 32 heady days.

For France 98, the tournament itself had been expanded from 24 to 32 participating nations for the first time. In his typical style, João Havelange had made the announcement of the tournament expansion on the eve of the 1994 FIFA Presidential election. Ambitiously, France 98 would therefore comprise of 64 matches to be played over one month. The first round would now be organised into eight groups of four teams, with two qualifiers from each group entering the knockout phase. Six seeded nations were chosen using a complex calculation that took into consideration current FIFA world rankings, performances at the previous three

World Cup tournaments, and FIFA world rankings in the corresponding years of 1986, 1990 and 1994. This led to the seeding of Germany, Italy, Spain, Argentina, Romania and the Netherlands, with holders Brazil and hosts France automatically seeded.

Ten venues were chosen to host the tournament, with £650 million committed to renovating nine stadiums and constructing the new Stade de France. *The World Soccer Essential Guide: France 98* detailed plans for each venue, and so what follows is largely from this useful resource.

Saint-Denis' Stade de France was the crown jewel of the project, purpose-built in the northern suburbs of Paris at a cost of £267 million. The impressive 80,000-capacity stadium included shops, restaurants, an exhibition hall, a cinema, training facilities and a 6,000-capacity car park. During the stadium's opening match, France versus Spain in January 1998, concerns immediately arose over the bumpy condition of the newly-laid pitch. These concerns led to intensive work on the surface in the months that followed to avoid embarrassment in the World Cup's opening match. The Stade de France was scheduled to host five group matches, one second-round match, one quarter-final and the World Cup Final on 12 July. This schedule, of course, included the opening match, Scotland versus holders Brazil, on 10 June.

Elsewhere, the 35,200-capacity Parc de Lescure in Bordeaux had been purpose-built for France's previous hosting of the World Cup finals in 1938, but for 1998 its refurbishment cost £6.2 million, which paid for seating added to the lower terraces and extensive new stadium facilities. Bordeaux was scheduled to host five group stage matches and one second-round match, including Scotland versus Norway on 16 June. RC Lens' 35,200-capacity Stade

Félix-Bollaert was a 65-year-old stadium that received a £14 million upgrade primarily to build new stands behind each goal. It was also scheduled to host five group matches and one-second round match. Lyon's 44,000-capacity Stade Gerland, at that time still the home of Olympique Lyonnais, was built in 1924, and had received two new stands and extensive modernisation of facilities at a cost of £8.7 million. Lyon was scheduled to host five group stage matches and one quarter-final. Olympique de Marseille's impressively rebuilt 60,000-capacity Stade Vélodrome received three new stands, a new tier added to the main stand and extensive stadium facilities, at a cost of £39 million. The Stade Vélodrome also hosted the World Cup draw in December 1997, and was scheduled to host four group-stage matches, one second-round match, one quarter-final and one semi-final. Montpellier's 35,500-capacity Stade de la Mosson got two new stands and extensive internal refitting at a cost of £9.4 million. Montpellier was scheduled to host five group matches and one second-round match. FC Nantes' 40,000-capacity Stade de la Beaujoire did not require alteration to its impressive curved structure, but had benefitted from plexiglass wind breaks and internal upgrades at a cost of £4.3 million. Nantes was scheduled to host five group-stage matches and one quarter-final. Paris's 49,000-capacity Parc des Princes, the home of Paris St Germain, was originally built in 1897 and rebuilt in 1932 and 1972 to accommodate both football and rugby. The Parc des Princes received a £5.4-million spend to improve press and disabled facilities, install VIP suites and add technical installations such as scoreboards and lights. The Parc des Princes was scheduled to host four group matches, one second-round match and the third-place play-off match. Saint-Etienne's 36,000-capacity Stade Geoffroy-Guichard received facilities upgrades and underwent conversion of open terraces to covered seating at a cost £9.8 million. This was despite the owners, AS Saint-Etienne, languishing in the French second division at the time. Saint-Etienne was scheduled to host five group matches and one second-round match, including Scotland versus Morocco on 23 June. Toulouse's 37,000-capacity Stadium de Toulouse had undergone a £17-million refit to add extra tiers, improve floodlighting and construct a service block to the rear of the stadium. Toulouse was scheduled to host five group matches and one second-round match.

But what of the teams who would grace these shiny new venues? We will hear much more about Scotland's Group A bedfellows in later chapters, but there were 28 other teams in Groups B to H, all with different journeys to France 98.

Group B

Group B comprised Italy, Chile, Cameroon and Austria, with matches taking place in Bordeaux, Toulouse, Saint-Etienne, Montpellier, Saint-Denis and Nantes. The seeded Italians had struggled somewhat in qualification, finishing second in their group behind Glenn Hoddle's England. This was despite famously beating England 1–0 at Wembley in February 1997, with Gianfranco Zola's goal inflicting England's first-ever home defeat in a World Cup qualifier. Their second-place group finish had plunged the Italians into a tricky two-legged play-off with Russia, which they had narrowly won 2–1 on aggregate following a winning goal from resurgent Lazio striker Pierluigi Casiraghi, written off at international level only months before.

The Italians were managed by former Milan defender Cesare Maldini, who had lifted the European Cup as Milan captain in 1963 (after defeating injured Craig Brown's Scottish champions Dundee in the semi-finals). As a player, Maldini had won 14 caps for Italy and was of course the father of Paolo, Italy's captain for France 98. Paolo Maldini, at age 29, was widely considered the best left back in the world and had already amassed 87 international caps and won a plethora of medals with Milan. Cesare Maldini had replaced another Milan legend Arigo Sacchi as national team coach in December 1996 following a poor Euro 96 showing in England. Sacchi had led Italy to the World Cup Final just two years earlier in the USA, but the football-obsessed Italians could not tolerate a first-round exit at a major tournament.

Cesare Maldini had been steeped in the *catenaccio* playing style of the 1960s discussed in the first chapter of this book, and favoured a defensive style with Milan's Alessandro Costacurta playing as a sweeper. Fabio Cannavaro and Alessandro Nesta had emerged as world-class defenders, and on paper Italy had arguably the best defence at France 98. In midfield and attack, Maldini had tinkered and tested but had yet to find a blend with which he was satisfied. An embarrassment of attacking riches included 23-year-old Alessandro Del Piero, top scorer in the 1997–98 Champions League with ten goals for Juventus, Roberto Baggio, star performer at the 1990 and 1994 World Cup tournaments, powerful striker Christian Vieri, recently transferred from Juventus to Atletico Madrid for £12.5 million, and Filippo 'Pippo' Inzaghi, scorer of 18 league goals for Juventus in their 1997–98 title-winning season. The plucky Italians, notoriously slow starters at major tournaments, were nevertheless considered among the favourites at odds of around 8–1 to win the World Cup.

Austria, of course, had won Scotland's qualification group, with Scotland's best qualifier performance coming in the 2–0 home victory over the Austrians in April 1997. In Scotland's first-ever World Cup match, Austria had beaten Scotland 1–0 in the first round of the 1954 tournament in Switzerland, where the Austrian *Wunderteam* achieved a third-place finish. Despite some impressive displays in France 98 qualification, Austria's team of 1998, however, were no *Wunderteam*, and were reliant on steady veterans who had featured at the 1990 World Cup.

Cameroon were also no longer the force who sent shockwaves through world football at the 1990 World Cup after beating Argentina in the opening match. The 'Indomitable Lions' of 1990 were the team who had come closest to fulfilling Pelé's famous prophecy that an African team would win the World Cup before the millennium. Now, in 1998, this prophecy looked more like a curse for the Africans, with the wonderful talents of African football often let down by alleged corruption within the football associations and leadership of the Confederation of African Football (CAF). World Cup hero of the past Roger Milla, the oldest player ever to score at the tournament, had now retired, and following a disruptive but predictable managerial change on the eve of the tournament, little was expected from Cameroon.

Chile on the other hand were tipped as a possible wildcard team for France 98. This was down to their world-class strike partnership of Iván Zamorano of Inter Milan and Marcelo Salas of River Plate (though he was set to join Lazio after the World Cup). Chile had finished fourth in the incredibly tough South American qualification table, enough for automatic qualification, and had finished on 32 goals, nine more than any other South American nation. Impressively, the 'ZaSa' partners also finished as top and second-top scorers in South American qualification, with Zamorano netting 12 and Salas netting eleven. Chile also had a third reputable striker in contention, this time with a Scottish connection. The unfortunate Seb Rozental of Rangers would almost certainly have travelled to France 98 had it not been for an injury-hit season in Scotland. Rozental had faced two knee operations in seven months and was not fit enough to be included in Chile's final 22-man squad.

As a football nation, Chile were still overcoming the ignominy of having been banned from the 1990 and 1994 World Cup finals due to the national team's shameful behaviour in a qualification match versus Brazil in Rio in 1989. The ban had been handed to the Chilean Football Association by FIFA after photographic evidence proved Chilean goalkeeper and captain Roberto Rojas had faked being hit by a smoke bomb thrown from the Maracanã crowd. It was alleged that Rojas, who emerged as a stricken, bleeding figure after the smoke bomb landed, had also cut himself with a razor hidden in his glove during the incident. Rojas was banned from football for life, and with him went a generation of Chilean footballers who missed the chance to play at a World Cup.

Group C

Group C comprised France, South Africa, Saudi Arabia and Denmark, with matches taking place in Lens, Marseille, Toulouse, Saint-Denis, Lyon and Bordeaux. Seeded as hosts, the French had participated in a series of preparatory friendly matches instead of qualifiers, including the aforementioned friendly match against Scotland in Saint-Etienne in November 1997, which France won 2–1. France were coached by former Lyon and AS Saint-Etienne midfielder Aimé Jacquet, who had succeeded Gérard Houllier as head coach in 1994. In his autobiography *The Game of My Life*, Craig Brown recalls Jacquet cut a slightly nervous figure in November 1997, apparently struggling under the weight of expectation as manager of the World Cup's host nation. Brown recollects that Jacquet was receiving fierce criticism from his countrymen at that point, with continual doubts cast over his leadership. It is possible Brown related to Jacquet's plight in this regard!

The greatest dilemma facing Jacquet on the eve of France 98 was whether his team would score enough goals at the tournament. It was undeniable that the French were blessed with world-class defenders and midfielders such as Laurent Blanc, Lilian Thuram, Zinedine Zidane, Didier Deschamps and Youri Djorkaeff. In Fabien Barthez, the French had also solved their goalkeeping problems. However, it was generally felt that the French were light in attack. To address this, two prodigious young talents from AS Monaco were included in the final squad. Thierry Henry and David Trezeguet, born just two months apart, were both only 20 years old, but had shot to prominence in France's top flight at just the right moment. A third young talent in contention had been Arsenal's 19-year-old striker Nicolas Anelka, who was tested in a 0–0 draw with Sweden in April 1998 but somewhat controversially missed the final cut.

Jacquet would therefore rely upon the enigmatic Christophe Dugarry, now at Marseille after unsuccessful spells at Barcelona and Milan, and Stephane Guivarc'h of Auxerre, top scorer in the French top flight for the last two seasons. Concerningly, the two strikers had scored only three international goals between them, with midfielder Djorkaeff the squad's top international scorer on 15 goals. Defender Laurent Blanc was the squad's second-top international goalscorer on 12, a statistic that must have further unnerved Jacquet. Goals were therefore expected to come from midfield, with French hopes pinned on the questionable temperament of Zinedine 'Zizou' Zidane of Juventus. Playmaker Zidane's on-field relationship with Djorkaeff had looked promising in the preparatory matches, and he had a good understanding with Dugarry from their early club days together at Bordeaux. Home advantage was also widely expected to help *Les Bleus*, with the bookmakers providing odds of around 7–1 for France to win the World Cup for the first time.

Elsewhere in Group C, Denmark were expected to give France the most trouble at the first-round stage. France 98, surprisingly, marked only Denmark's second appearance at the World Cup finals, after the 'Danish Dynamite' side of World Cup 1986. The only survivor of this exciting team was 33-year-old Michael Laudrup, now of Ajax, who with younger brother Brian, of Rangers, and goalkeeper Peter Schmeichel, of Manchester United, were Denmark's three world-class players. Schmeichel and the younger Laudrup were survivors of Denmark's remarkable Euro 92 win in Sweden. Michael, arguably Denmark's most talented ever player, had not been part of their greatest international success in 1992, due to a dispute with head coach at the time, Richard Møller Nielsen. In Schmeichel, many felt Denmark had the world's best goalkeeper, and the Danes' squad also included centre-back Marc Rieper and midfielder Morten

Wieghorst, both important members of Celtic's 1997–98 title-winning squad.

Group C's two outsiders were Saudi Arabia and South Africa. Saudi Arabia's only previous appearance at the finals had been four years earlier in the USA, where they had beaten Belgium and Morocco to qualify for the second round, before being eliminated by Sweden. Saudi Arabia's run to the second round was considered one of the biggest shocks in World Cup history, and their winning goal against Belgium, a solo run by Saeed Al-Owairan, is considered one of the greatest World Cup goals ever scored. Owairan, a former Asian Footballer of the Year, was included in Saudi Arabia's France 98 squad despite having lost the preceding two years of his football career after being caught at an illegal alcohol party in 1995 and found guilty of 'immoral acts' under Saudi Arabian law, leading to a prison sentence and 18-month football ban.

Due to the Saudi success of 1994, the oil-rich state had high expectations of their team at France 98 and had appointed Brazilian Carlos Alberto Parreira as head coach. Parreira was taking charge of his fourth nation at a World Cup finals, after Kuwait in 1982, the United Arab Emirates in 1990 and Brazil in 1994, whom he had led to victory in the USA. While some may have viewed the relative success of the Saudi Arabians of this era as a fluke, this would be inaccurate. Considerable money had been poured into Saudi Arabian football over a long period, and as beaten finalists, Scotland in particular will never forget Saudi Arabia's victory in the Under-16 World Cup Final at Hampden Park in 1989.

Slightly less was expected of World Cup debutants South Africa, who did not play their first international football match until 1992, due to their exclusion from FIFA as a consequence of their government's apartheid policy. Nevertheless, the South Africans had performed unexpectedly well at the recent Africa Cup of Nations held in Burkina Faso in February 1998, reaching the final, where they were beaten by Egypt, who themselves had not qualified for France 98. Furthermore, in 20-year-old Benni McCarthy of Ajax, South Africa had unearthed a footballer with superstar potential. With South Africa having played out two mediocre draws in their opening group matches, McCarthy spectacularly sprang to life in their third match against Namibia. Incredibly, McCarthy scored four goals in 13 minutes against the Namibians, which was also South Africa's first ever hat-trick at international level. McCarthy finished the 1998 Africa Cup of Nations as player of the tournament, and as joint-top scorer with prolific Egyptian Hossam Hassan on seven goals.

Group D

Group D comprised Spain, Nigeria, Paraguay and Bulgaria, with matches taking place in Montpellier, Nantes, Saint-Etienne, Paris, Lens and Toulouse. In 1998, seeded Spain held the reputation as the serial underachievers of international football. Managed by tough-talking head coach Javier Clemente, whose own promising career with Athletic Bilbao had been cruelly cut short by injury, Spain were as usual tipped by many to go all the way at France 98. Faith in Spain's chances was reinforced by their excellent qualification form as they emerged unbeaten from a group containing Yugoslavia and the Czech Republic. The strength of Spain's qualification group is perhaps best illustrated by the elimination of the strong Czechs, who had reached the final of Euro 96 just two years before.

Spain, competing in their sixth consecutive World Cup, had undoubted quality in their squad, but an injury to midfield linchpin Pep Guardiola concerned Clemente. In an interview with *World Soccer* shortly before France 98, Clemente stated that he had 'special qualities', a 'style of his own [that] is impossible to find in other players' and 'offers us tactical variation which nobody else can supply'. This tactical variation was Guardiola positioned alongside versatile Real Madrid centre-back Fernando Hierro, who operated as a defensive midfielder for Spain. Without Guardiola's passing and playmaking abilities, and no adequate available replacement, Clemente undoubtedly feared his midfield was weakened beyond repair. Spain of 1998 were a direct team who preferred quickly to turn defence into attack, which may be inconceivable to those raised on Spain's ultra-possession-based 'tiki-taka' style that came to prominence a decade later. As head coach of Barcelona, Guardiola was of course central to this tactical revolution, which reflected his own playing style.

For flair, Clemente relied on 20-year-old Real Madrid protégé Raúl, who alongside Hierro was fresh from Real Madrid's 1997–98 Champions League win, the club's first triumph in Europe's top club competition since 1965–66. Clemente had been widely criticised for omitting Raúl from his Euro 96 squad, but his worried interviews in the lead-up to France 98 suggested he would not make the same mistake twice.

Group D also contained Nigeria, the pick of the four competing African nations, and a team many head coaches had been keen to avoid in the first round. Nigeria were managed by Serbian Bora Milutinović, who, like Carlos Alberto Parreira, was taking charge of his fourth nation at a World Cup finals. Milutinović had a wealth of World

Cup experience, having taken charge of hosts Mexico in 1986 and then hosts the USA in 1994. As head coach of Costa Rica in 1990, Milutinović had also been the architect of Scotland's lowest ebb at the World Cup finals. In the perpetual managerial merry-go-round of the African and CONCACAF nations, Milutinović had successfully steered Mexico to France 98, only to be dismissed in December 1997. Milutinović then replaced Frenchman Phillippe Troussier as Nigerian head coach, after Troussier had faced a similar fate following successful France 98 qualification with the Nigerians. Incidentally, this is not where the story ended for Troussier, who booked his own personal passage to the World Cup finals after taking charge of South Africa in early 1998. The odd man out in this game of managerial musical chairs was the unfortunate Jomo Sono, who as caretaker had done a remarkable job in steering South Africa to the final of the Africa Cup of Nations in February 1998, only to be replaced by Troussier.

Opponents feared the Nigerian 'Super Eagles' of 1998 mainly due to their exploits at the previous World Cup in 1994, where they had been very unfortunate to exit in the second round after late heroics by Italian Roberto Baggio, who scored an extra-time penalty with the score at 1–1 to break Nigerian hearts. Typically, despite the talents of Europe-based stars such as Nwankwo Kanu of Inter Milan, Jay-Jay Okocha of Fenerbahçe and Tijani Babangida of Ajax, political troubles had caused Nigeria to be removed from the 1996 Africa Cup of Nations, though this had not prevented them winning the gold medal at the Atlanta Olympics in the same year. Even in 1998, things were not straightforward, and *World Soccer* highlighted that on the eve of France 98 the squad were still in a pay dispute with the Nigerian Football Association, undermining their World Cup preparations.

Group D also featured Bulgaria, another of the surprise teams of USA 94. France 98 would be Bulgaria's eighth appearance at the World Cup finals, but until 1994 they had never won a match at the finals. Their glorious run in the USA ultimately ended in semi-final defeat by Italy, with that man Roberto Baggio again stealing the show with both goals in a 2–1 win for Italy. At France 98, ageing talisman Hristo Stoichkov, who had finished USA 94 as joint-top goalscorer with the enigmatic Russian ex-Rangers striker Oleg Salenko on six goals, would lead Bulgaria. European Footballer of the Year in 1994 Stoichkov, now aged 32, had returned to CSKA Sofia from Barcelona after being dropped by Barcelona head coach Louis Van Gaal. Several other Bulgarian heroes of USA 94 were also now in their 30s, including Krassimir Balakov and Emil Kostadinov. The omission of Yordan Letchkov, scorer of their famous winner against Germany in the quarter-finals of USA 94, compounded the general sense that this was a tournament too far for Bulgaria's golden generation. Letchkov was without a club after leaving Beşiktaş and so ultimately missed the final 22-man squad.

Paraguay were the fourth team in Group D, and were undoubtedly at the finals on merit, having finished an impressive second-best in South American qualification, with only Argentina amassing more than their 29 points. In charismatic goalkeeper José Luis Chilavert, Paraguay also possessed one of football's true icons of the era. Twice voted the best goalkeeper in the world, Chilavert had also scored four international goals, including a vital equalising free kick in a 1–1 away draw against Argentina during qualification. Led by Chilavert, it was anticipated that Paraguay would continue in their defensive style at France 98 and be difficult opponents to break down.

Group E

Group E comprised the Netherlands, Belgium, South Korea and Mexico, with matches taking place in Lyon, Saint-Denis, Bordeaux, Marseille, Saint-Etienne and Paris. With abundant talent in their 22-man squad, twice World Cup runners-up the Netherlands were the seeded team in Group E. They were managed by former PSV Eindhoven manager Guus Hiddink, who had led PSV to European Cup victory ten years earlier in 1988, the same year as the Netherlands' only major international tournament victory at Euro 88. An equally talented crop of young players, mostly reaching their peak as France 98 beckoned, had replaced the stars of Euro 88 such as Ruud Gullit, Marco van Basten and Frank Rijkaard.

Louis Van Gaal's Ajax team that conquered Europe in 1995, and came close to doing so again in 1996 as beaten finalists, made up the spine of the Netherlands' international first eleven. Of the team who won the Champions League with Ajax in 1995, Edwin van der Sar, Michael Reiziger, Winston Bogarde, Frank de Boer, Clarence Seedorf, Edgar Davids, Ronald de Boer, Marc Overmars and Patrick Kluivert were all expected to be in and around the Netherlands' starting line-up. Dennis Bergkamp, PFA and FWA Player of the Year in 1998 with Arsene Wenger's double-winning Arsenal, and the world's most expensive defender, Manchester United's Jaap Stam, were also expected starters. With proven quality in every position, the Dutch were undoubtedly among the favourites to win the World Cup in 1998, but many questioned whether they could overcome the squad harmony problems which derailed their Euro 96 efforts. Following Edgar Davids' superb form with Juventus, who had won Serie A and reached the Champions League final in 1997–98, Hiddink had sensibly now resolved his difficulties with Davids and recalled him for France 98. Hiddink would most certainly be trying to avoid a repeat of the infighting that had led to Davids being sent home early from the Euros.

Twenty-one-year-old star striker Patrick Kluivert had also had a torrid time since shooting to fame as an 18-year-old in 1995 after scoring the winning goal for Ajax in the Champions League final. Kluivert had since transferred from Ajax to Milan, but had failed to live up to his promise in his first (and what would be only) season in Italy. Aside from his somewhat disappointing form, Kluivert had been found guilty of death by dangerous driving in 1996 after his involvement in a fatal car accident, and in 1997 was accused of rape, charges which were eventually dismissed in the Amsterdam court of appeal in February 1998 due to insufficient evidence. Correspondingly, in their pre-tournament profile of the Netherlands, *World Soccer*'s headline simply read, 'Struggling with the demons: the Dutch may again prove their own worst enemies.'

Belgium, competing at their fifth consecutive World Cup, were expected to be the Netherlands' main rivals in Group E. The neighbouring nations, having also emerged from the same France 98 qualification group, had again been drawn to face each other at the finals, the only occurrence of this in the World Cup 1998 draw. Strangely, Belgium and the Netherlands seemingly could not escape each other during this period, having also been drawn in the same group at World Cup USA 94. The Dutch had ultimately pipped the Belgians to the post during France 98 qualification, with Belgium finishing on 18 points, one point behind the Netherlands' 19. This had required Belgium to play off against the Republic of Ireland, with Belgium winning 3–2 on aggregate.

Belgium of this era were not blessed with the same strength in depth of later generations, and due to midfield shortages they had recalled 37-year-old veteran Franky Van der Elst during qualification. This had followed the sacking of Wilfried Van Moer after a 3–0 home defeat by the Netherlands (who else?) and the subsequent appointment of former Club Brugge defender Georges Leekens as head coach in December 1996. Leekens had thereafter steadied the ship, and Belgium were generally felt to have good options in forward positions, with Brazil-born naturalised Belgian Luís Oliviera of Fiorentina and Luc Nilis of PSV Eindhoven expected to partner each other in attack. Van der Elst, along with cultured midfielder Enzo Scifo, were survivors of Belgium's Mexico 86 squad, who had achieved their best-ever finish at a World Cup at that time, in fourth place.

The third nation in Group E were South Korea, playing in their fourth consecutive World Cup, and their fifth overall. South Korea were managed by their greatest-ever player, Cha Bum-kun, who had played 308 times and scored 98 goals in the Bundesliga for Eintracht Frankfurt and Bayer Leverkusen between 1979 and 1989. Possibly the first pioneer of contemporary Asian football, Bum-kun was capped 136 times and scored 58 goals for South Korea during an equally impressive international career, which included appearances at Mexico 86. Bum-kun, a renowned disciplinarian according to *World Soccer*, did not have any players available to him who matched his own impressive playing CV, but had nonetheless comfortably steered South Korea to qualification from the Asian group sections. In 1998, South Korea had already been named as co-hosts for the 2002 World Cup, which was in no small part due to the influence of South Korean FIFA Executive Committee member and Hyundai billionaire Chung Mong-Joon. France 98 therefore felt like something of a dress rehearsal for the South Koreans, who already had one eye on co-hosting the tournament four years later.

The fourth nation comprising Group E were twice World Cup hosts Mexico. Playing in their eleventh World Cup finals, Mexico had only won a disappointing seven of their 33 matches at the finals, with their best quarter-final finishes coming as hosts in 1970 and 1986. In *How They Stole the Game*, David Yallop theorises that former FIFA President João Havelange's dealings with Mexican media magnate and billionaire Emilio Azcárraga were the deciding factor in poverty-stricken Mexico landing two World Cups just 16 years apart. Perpetually under the influence of Azcárraga's monopolising media company Televisa, which also owned multiple Mexican football clubs, Mexico's France 98 omission of Cruz Azul players (a club not owned by Televisa) appeared questionable, according to *World Soccer*. The most glaring omission was that of record national team goalscorer Carlos Hermosillo, top scorer in qualification with ten goals. After securing qualification, Mexico had also controversially replaced head coach Bora Milutinović with ex-Necaxa striker Manuel Lapuente in December 1997, further disrupting squad preparations. Since the retirement of star striker Hugo Sánchez, who had starred at club level for Real Madrid, Mexico now looked to blond-haired striker Luis Hernández to fill the void. Hernández and flamboyant goalkeeper Jorge Campos were Mexico's most recognisable players in their 22-man squad.

Group F

Group F comprised Germany, Yugoslavia, Iran and the USA, with matches taking place in Saint-Etienne, Paris, Lens, Lyon, Montpellier and Nantes. The seeded nation in Group F were of course three-time winners Germany, who, as West Germany, had previously triumphed in 1954, 1974 and 1990. Germany were also reigning European champions, having won Euro 96 two years earlier in England, albeit with a somewhat unmemorable team by their exceptional standards. Head coach Berti Vogts unsurprisingly remained in charge following the Euro win, but Germany had laboured slightly in qualification, and in their final qualifier had trailed at home to Albania, a result which would have caused them to miss out on automatic qualification. Inevitably, Germany, masters of the late comeback, had dug deep on more than one occasion during qualification, relying primarily on the late goals of super substitute Oliver Bierhoff of Udinese. Bierhoff, hero of the Euro 96 final at Wembley, was set to join Milan after France 98, after finishing the 1997–98 season as top scorer in Serie A.

World Cup winners Jürgen Kohler, Stefan Reuter, Olaf Thon, Lothar Matthäus, Thomas Hässler and Jürgen Klinsmann remained in their squad. Those who participated at Italia 90, where Germany were deserved victors, were arguably now mostly past their peak. But despite Germany travelling to France 98 with an ageing squad, their proven track record and never-say-die mentality placed them among the tournament favourites, as always.

Yugoslavia, the other nation expected to qualify from Group F, were competing at their first major tournament since Italia 90, where coincidentally they had also faced Germany in the group stage. Yugoslavia, who would finally become Serbia and Montenegro in 2003, had been banned from international football for two and a half years due to their role in the Balkan conflict. This meant Yugoslavia and several of their stars playing in European football had missed out on Euro 92, USA 94 and Euro 96.

Yugoslavia had finished second to Spain in their qualification group, before crushing Hungary 12–1 on aggregate in a two-legged play-off. Star forward Predrag Mijatović scored an incredible seven of Yugoslavia's 12 play-off goals, and when added to his seven from the group stage, Mijatović finished as Europe's top qualification scorer on 14 goals. Mijatović had also recently written himself into the football history books by scoring the only goal of the 1998 Champions League final for Real Madrid against Juventus. Yugoslavia also had another player of considerable stature in Milan's Dejan Savićević, who for many had been Man of the Match in the 1994 Champions League final when Milan unexpectedly thrashed Johan Cruyff's Barcelona 4–0 in Athens. Talented captain Dragan Stojković, survivor of Yugoslavia's 1990 World Cup team, added tournament experience to the squad, and Lazio-bound 19-year-old Dejan Stanković added youth. On paper, Yugoslavia certainly had the talent to do well at France 98, and for many were another possible wildcard pick.

In a quirk of fate, ideological enemies Iran and the USA were the other two nations drawn in Group F. Due to their political differences, and the expected gulf in class between themselves and Germany and Yugoslavia, the USA and Iran were firmly focused on each other in Group F. The USA, hosts four years before, were competing in their third consecutive World Cup. Head coach Steve Sampson had been assistant to Bora Milutinović in 1994 when the USA commendably reached the second round on home soil. In terms of players, the USA possessed two excellent goalkeepers in Leicester City's Kasey Keller and Liverpool's Brad Friedel. Much was also expected of future Rangers player Claudio Reyna, playing in the Bundesliga at the time. For goals, the USA relied upon record national team goalscorer Eric Wynalda. Sampson appeared keen to play attacking football at France 98, but it was generally felt that the USA lacked the strength in depth to emerge from Group F.

Iran were playing in their second World Cup, having previously featured at World Cup 1978 in Argentina. Drawn with Scotland at the group stages of Argentina 78, Scotland will never forget Iran's only World Cup point to date, a 1–1 draw with 'Ally's Army' in Córdoba. This result had followed Scotland's 3–1 crushing by Peru, and firmly burst the bubble of ill-prepared manager Ally MacLeod and his claims that Scotland would win the World Cup. This time around, Iran had qualified via a two-legged Asia-Oceania play-off with Australia, who were managed by England's Euro 96 manager Terry Venables at the time. An impressive 130,000 spectators had attended Iran's home leg versus Australia in Tehran, a record in the France 98 qualifiers, and midfielder Karim Bagheri was the highest qualification scorer across all continents with 18 goals in 13 matches. Overall, Iran were reliant on their trio of German Bundesliga-based players for inspiration: Bagheri and Ali Daei of Arminia Bielefeld, and Khodadad Azizi of FC Köln. According to *World Soccer*, Venables referred to Australia's loss to Iran as his worst-ever experience in football.

Group G

Group G comprised Romania, Colombia, England and Tunisia, with matches taking place in Marseille, Lyon,

Montpellier, Toulouse, Saint-Denis and Lens. The seeded nation in Group G were Romania – not England, as many would have assumed on paper. This was also not the first time Romania and England had faced each other in the first round of the World Cup, with England overcoming Romania 1–0 in the group stage of Mexico 70, thanks to a goal from Geoff Hurst.

Romania had been surprising quarter-finalists at World Cup USA 94, and had easily won their France 98 qualification group, finishing ten points ahead of the second-placed Republic of Ireland. That said, they had not fared well at Euro 96 in England two years earlier, losing all three group matches with only one goal scored in total. At France 98, Romania were still led by their greatest-ever player, Gheorghe Hagi, now of Galatasaray, and many of his USA 94 team-mates were also still available. Players such as Gheorghe Popescu, Hagi's clubmate at Galatasaray, Chelsea's Dan Petrescu, and Ilie Dumitrescu, who had played in England for both Tottenham Hotspur and West Ham. World Cup 1990 veteran Marius Lacatus was also included, with much expected of promising £7 million Valencia striker Adrian Ilie. Another star of USA 94, ex-Milan striker Florin Răducioiu, had now retired from international football, weakening Romania's attack. But with plenty of major tournament experience, Romania were expected to provide their usual stiff opposition, and it was worth noting that it had taken penalties to eliminate them at both Italia 90 and USA 94.

As arguably the strongest of the unseeded nations, England were the other team expected to qualify from Group G. Following heartbreak at Euro 96 after a gallingly familiar semi-final defeat to Germany on penalties, England were now under the interesting leadership of one of their most talented ever players, Glenn Hoddle. As a player, skilful midfielder Hoddle had won 53 caps for England, and at club level had played for Tottenham Hotspur and Monaco, where he had won the French title under future Arsenal boss Arsène Wenger. *World Soccer* asserts that Wenger strongly influenced Hoddle's decision to move into football management at the end of his playing career. By 1998, Wenger was considered one of the best managers in the world, having just led Arsenal to the league and cup double playing superb football. When speaking to Andy Brassell on the *Football Ramble* podcast, Wenger commented that Hoddle 'was a fantastic football player, and had that quality, right and left foot, to play that ball in behind defenders. And he scored goals.'

Hoddle was praised in the English press after England topped their qualification group ahead of Italy, successfully playing the Italians at their own game to draw 0–0 in Rome in October 1997 to earn the single point they required in their final group match. Conversely, as France 98 approached, Hoddle's press profile was no longer as positive, with his spiritual beliefs coming under intense scrutiny. This had followed revelations that Hoddle had included faith healer Eileen Drewery as part of his France 98 travelling delegation, a fact that had not played out well for Hoddle in the English tabloids. When speaking to the *Sunday Express*, Hoddle stated that at the two World Cups he'd played at in 1982 and 1986, he felt they'd neglected 'details the Germans, Italians and Brazilians pay so much attention to', meaning 'things like diet, physical preparation and, most importantly, getting the players' minds totally focused'. In response to pressing questions on his opinions about religion, Hoddle reportedly gestured towards the training ground and said, 'This is my church'.

Whatever Hoddle's outlook, faith in England's chances was backed up by the most exciting crop of English players to emerge for some time. Four 23-year-old members of Manchester United's famous 'Class of 92' were in the squad: David Beckham, Paul Scholes, Gary Neville and Nicky Butt. Gary's younger brother, the versatile Phil Neville, aged only 21, was also included in the final 22-man squad.

In Newcastle United's Alan Shearer, England also had one of the best strikers in the world. After finishing as top scorer at Euro 96, and with a vital winner against France in England's victory at the 1997 Tournoi de France round-robin competition, where Brazil and Italy were the other two competing teams, Shearer had now proven he could score goals at the very highest level. Add to this the emergence of the electric 18-year-old Michael Owen of Liverpool, and Manchester United's clever front man Teddy Sheringham, and England had plenty of ammunition in attack – so much so, that English Premier League top scorer Andy Cole of Manchester United hadn't even made the final 22-man squad. In defence, England were also fairly settled, with Tony Adams and Sol Campell sure starters, and Gary Neville and Gareth Southgate interchangeable as the third member of a back three.

Ironically, for ex-midfielder Hoddle, it was in midfield where most question marks remained for England. Beckham was the only player who had started every France 98 qualification match, but playing as a right wing-back, where many felt his midfield prowess was wasted. Hoddle had also been required to solve the conundrum created by the personal difficulties of Paul Gascoigne, undoubtedly the most talented English footballer of his generation. On the eve of France 98, *World Soccer* referred to Gascoigne as England's major creative source, but perhaps an accident waiting to happen. In the end, Hoddle did controversially omit him from his France 98 squad. Rather like Craig Brown with Ally McCoist, the reason Hoddle officially offered for dropping Gascoigne was his questionable fitness level, but it is possible Hoddle simply did not trust Gascoigne in the squad environment. Let us also not forget that Gascoigne's creative midfield berth would instead be occupied by the wonderfully talented Scholes, and with experienced midfield enforcers Paul Ince and David Batty included, England appeared to have all bases covered, without risking the problems that might have followed Gascoigne to France.

Led by inspirational 36-year-old midfielder Carlos Valderrama, the third nation drawn in Group G were Colombia. Like several other stars of previous World Cups, France 98 would be the final tournament for Colombia's captain with his distinctive blond hairstyle. Nonetheless, Valderrama was a lot more than a hairstyle, and in *A Bhoy's Own Story*, with reference to Scotland's pre-tournament 2-2 draw with the Colombians, Paul Lambert described Valderrama as a terrific player with a great touch, despite his age. For Colombia to succeed at France 98, a lot would also depend on the fitness of their star striker Faustino Asprilla of Parma, who had been struggling with injury on the eve of the tournament. For Colombia, France 98 could not possibly be worse than their national catastrophe four years earlier in the USA, where they had capitulated in their first two matches after being strongly fancied as one of the pre-tournament favourites. Football will also never forget the brutal murder of defender Andres Escobar on his return home to Colombia in 1994, a crime apparently motivated by his own goal scored in Colombia's group stage loss to the USA.

The fourth and perhaps weakest team in Group G

were African qualifiers Tunisia. The Tunisians were managed by former Polish international Henryk Kasperczak, who had played at two World Cups with Poland, including in their third-place finish at West Germany 74. France 98 would be Tunisia's second appearance at the World Cup finals, after a credible showing at Argentina 78, where they had drawn with West Germany and beaten Mexico 3–1 to become the first African nation to win a World Cup match. Interestingly, head coach Kasperczak played for Poland in Tunisia's only loss at Argentina 78, where their one win and one draw were not enough for second-round qualification. Tunisia were not expected to reach similar heights at France 98, with their hopes pinned upon Zoubier Beya and Mehdi Bel Slimane of German club Freiburg, and striker Adel Sellimi of Nantes. In truth, the draw had not been kind to the Tunisians, with three formidable opponents waiting for them in Group G.

Group H

Group H comprised Argentina, Japan, Jamaica and Croatia, with matches taking place in Toulouse, Lens, Nantes, Paris, Bordeaux and Lyon. Argentina, managed by their 1978 World Cup-winning captain Daniel Passarella, were the seeded nation in Group H. In the lead-up to the tournament, *World Soccer* state that disciplinarian Passarella had made headlines for his tough stance on the appearance of his players – for example, making star striker Gabriel Batistuta of Fiorentina cut his long hair prior to joining the squad. Passarella's militaristic ways had already proved too much for long-haired midfielder Fernando Redondo. Despite winning the Champions League with Real Madrid in May 1998, Redondo refused to cut his hair to conform with Passarella's regime and so did not travel to France.

Despite Redondo's omission, Argentina were nonetheless blessed with an embarrassment of riches in their squad, with Passarella's headache how to blend the quality on offer. Centre-back Roberto Ayala (Napoli), wing-back Javier Zanetti (Inter Milan), midfield enforcer Diego Simeone (Inter Milan) and the powerful Juan Sebastián Verón (Sampdoria) were all sure starters. Another was their leading goalscorer and appearance maker in qualification, the diminutive Ariel Ortega of Valencia, the latest player saddled with the unhelpful 'new Maradona' tag. Passarella's main difficulty had been the form of his star strikers, none of whom had so far been able to capture their club form at international level. The strikers in contention were Claudio López (Valencia), Abel Balbo (Roma), Hernán Crespo (Parma) and the aforementioned Batistuta. It was widely acknowledged that if Argentina got it right at France 98, they had a realistic chance of their third World Cup triumph after their success as hosts in 1978 and at Mexico 86.

The second nation expected to emerge from Group H was Croatia, who were playing at their first World Cup finals. Head coach Miroslav Blažević was nonetheless treated with amused scepticism on the eve of the tournament, due to his seemingly over-confident predictions. Blažević told *World Soccer*, 'I'm convinced that we are ready for something big, and it will happen in France. I admire the French in many respects, and when I was coach of Nantes, I helped the development of some of their players. They [France] will get to the final. And so will we.'

While few shared Blažević's incredible optimism about Croatia's chances at France 98, there was little doubt they possessed players of the highest quality. Prolific striker

Davor Šuker was fresh from winning the 1998 Champions League with Real Madrid, albeit as a last-minute substitute in the final. In Zvonimir Boban of Milan and Robert Prosinečki, formerly of Barcelona and Real Madrid, Croatia also had top-class midfielders. The main difficulty for Croatia would be coping with the late withdrawal of Alen Bokšić of Lazio, star performer and hero of their qualification campaign with four goals, whose serious knee injury denied him his place in Croatia's squad.

The third nation in Group H were Japan, also competing at their first World Cup finals. Japan had come close to qualifying for USA 94, only to end up heartbroken after losing an unexpected last-minute goal to Iraq that allowed South Korea to qualify instead. For Japan, it had been important to qualify on merit for France 98, as they would be co-hosting the tournament with South Korea four years later. Japan's entire France 98 squad comprised players from their own increasingly successful J-League and, in 21-year-old Hidetoshi Nakata, Japan had potentially unearthed their first football superstar. National icon Nakata had been instrumental in Japan's historic one-legged Asian play-off victory over Iran in Malaysia in November 1997, with three assists in their 3–2 victory that secured World Cup qualification for the first time.

Jamaica, the fourth team in Group H, were possibly the biggest surprise qualifier for France 98. The 'Reggae Boyz' were also the third team in Group H competing at their first World Cup finals, providing a uniquely interesting contest, with one first-time entrant guaranteed to enter the knockout phase. Jamaica had successfully emerged from the CONCACAF qualification region under the management of Brazilian head coach René Simões, consequently now a Jamaican national hero. With cricket the predominant sport on the island, as recently as 1986 Jamaica had declined to compete in World Cup qualification due to their football association being unable to pay the entry fee. Simões, appointed in 1994, had professionalised and galvanised Jamaican football with his policy of combining English Premier League players, eligible through their parents or grandparents, with players from the Jamaican league. Frank Sinclair (Chelsea), Fitzroy Simpson (Portsmouth), Darryl Powell (Derby County), Robbie Earle (Wimbledon), Marcus Gayle (Wimbledon), Deon Burton (Derby County) and Paul Hall (Portsmouth) were all in this category, and between them had played a considerable number of matches at the highest level of English football. Prior to the tournament, Simões had also embarked upon a 25-five-match global warm-up tour to prepare his squad, eclipsing the preparations of most other competing nations. Despite their major tournament inexperience, nobody was writing off the chances of Simões' Jamaica grabbing a place in the knockout phase.

8

A SPACESHIP ON TAP AE IT

The ever-diligent Craig Brown had taken the opportunity to travel to Miami in February 1998 to watch Scotland's first World Cup opponents Brazil face Jamaica in the CONCACAF Gold Cup, a game that had finished 0–0. Brown's considered approach was in stark contrast to the farcical preparations of World Cups of the past, like Ally MacLeod turning down the opportunity to travel with BBC Sport to analyse Peru versus Argentina in Lima in March 1978, just three months before the Peruvians humiliated Scotland in Córdoba. By now, Brown had also watched two matches and attended a coaching workshop in the new purpose-built Stade de France, the awe-inspiring venue for the World Cup opener.

On the morning of Monday 8 June, Craig Brown sat on his balcony at the Valrugues Hotel, busily working on whiteboard football tactics. He had already picked his starting eleven for the Brazil match, but he had not yet informed the squad of his choices. Down below, his players relaxed at the poolside, reading newspapers and chatting, or taking refreshments with a game of pool indoors. It was a beautiful day in the picturesque St Rémy, and the atmosphere in the Scotland camp remained relaxed and positive. Later, Brown and Alex Miller led a closed training session in the bright sunshine. Brown's squad, in their white Scottish Gas-sponsored Umbro training tops and black shorts, completed familiar passing exercises and repetitive practice of corners and free kicks. Separately, Alan Hodgkinson coached the three Scotland goalkeepers, Jim Leighton, Neil Sullivan and Jonathan Gould. Overall, Brown was pleased with the fitness, motivation and attitude within the squad, and Scotland had sustained no noteworthy injuries since arriving in France.

Also available to participate in the training sessions were four 'hamper boys', who were Scotland Under-21 internationals selected to assist the squad and gain experience. The four were Mark Burchill (Celtic), Kieran McAnespie (St Johnstone), Darren Young (Aberdeen) and goalkeeper Paul Gallacher (Dundee United). Speaking of this experience 22 years later on the *Well Done Michael, He's 13* podcast, Young provided a fascinating insight into his experience as a France 98 hamper boy. Young confirmed that he and the others undertook mundane tasks such as arranging kits, boots and cones, but also trained with the squad frequently, participating in all aspects of Scotland's France 98 training sessions, such as shaping, crossing, shooting, defending and set-piece routines. Young also waited behind to assist players in extra ball work when training was over. He described his experience in France as very similar to the 22-man squad's, travelling with the delegation to every France 98 destination and attending team meetings and tactics sessions, where Craig Brown named his starting eleven for the matches. Young confirmed that this was a tremendous experience for an up-and-coming young player.

Darren Young would therefore have remembered the evening of 8 June at Scotland's base camp. Craig Brown had called an eagerly-anticipated team meeting in the lounge area, for the primary purpose of naming the starting line-up to face Brazil in the opening match of the World Cup. With the curtains drawn, which dimmed the room slightly, the players sat in rows facing a tactics flipchart, waiting in expectation for the big announcement. Brown stood at the front of the room and addressed his players, first discussing match tactics in detail. In his typical style, Brown had been working diligently in the preceding period, as he attempted to create a tactical plan that would foil the best player in the world at the time, Ronaldo.

In a 2019 interview with *Open Goal*, Brown disclosed that he phoned ex-England manager Bobby Robson for advice during his tactical preparations. Robson had managed Ronaldo at both PSV Eindhoven and Barcelona, so was the ideal candidate to advise Brown on how to handle the player nicknamed *O Fenômeno* ('The Phenomenon'). Brown recalled that Robson had said, 'He is the best striker I have ever had, and I have had a few. I've had Careca. I've had Romário. I've had Lineker. I've had all these guys. This guy is exceptional.' In response, Brown, seeking hope, recalled asking Robson if he should man-mark Ronaldo. 'No chance,' replied Robson, 'if you man-mark him, he will just roll your marker.' With a hint of desperation, Brown recollected asking Robson, 'So what do I do, Bobby?' Robson simply replied, 'Analyse Brazil's recent matches to see who he receives the ball from, and stop the supply to him!'

Brown therefore did exactly that, analysing nine Brazil matches, two of which he attended in person. In doing so, he learned that Ronaldo received most of his passes from right-back Cafu, who had been part of Brazil's 1994 World

Cup-winning side. Brown identified that Cafu would execute precise, low-driven passes to Ronaldo's feet, which acted as the star striker's primary supply chain. Brown correspondingly picked Christian Dailly to man-mark Cafu, with a stern warning issued to Dailly that if Cafu successfully passed to Ronaldo, he would be substituted! Brown was also quoted in the *Press & Journal* as saying he had also identified that left-back Roberto Carlos occasionally offered dangerous lofted passes to Ronaldo, but overall Cafu was definitely Ronaldo's main creative source, and that Dunga and the rest of Brazil's midfield were not his suppliers.

In terms of Brazil's other main threats, Paul Lambert recalls in *A Bhoy's Own Story* that Brown and Miller had gradually introduced their footage of the Brazilians in the days that preceded the team announcement. Lambert had studied the footage carefully, and had identified that he would predominantly be in the same area of the pitch as Rivaldo, another superstar of the era. Lambert now relished pitting himself against the best in the world, after spectacularly resurrecting his own stuttering career as a pioneer of the landmark 1995 Jean-Marc Bosman 'freedom of movement' ruling. Lambert's unlikely conversion, from forgotten attacking midfielder with Motherwell to world-class defensive midfielder and Champions League-winner with Borussia Dortmund, is one of Scottish football's great stories. Craig Brown had also become increasingly impressed with the previously forgotten ex-captain of Scotland's Under-21s. Indeed, at the World Cup draw in December 1997, Brown recalled that Germany manager Berti Vogts had informed him that Lambert would definitely have been selected for Germany's France 98 squad, had he been German. High praise indeed, considering that

Germany were reigning European champions and one of the tournament favourites.

Among the players, the main surprise of the team announcement was the attacking nature of the line-up, which included Darren Jackson, Kevin Gallacher and Gordon Durie. Craig Burley, continuing in his right wing-back role, as opposed to the midfield role which saw him win the Scottish Football Writers' Association Player of the Year award with Celtic, was the other major talking point. Lambert recollects that, overall, the team were pleased with the line-up and quietly confident.

The full Scotland team named to face Brazil on 10 June 1998 was as follows, in order of squad numbers: Jim Leighton (1); Tom Boyd (3); Colin Calderwood (4); Colin Hendry (5); Kevin Gallacher (7); Craig Burley (8); Gordon Durie (9); Darren Jackson (10); John Collins (11); Paul Lambert (14); Christian Dailly (22).

Tuesday 9 June was another beautiful day in St Rémy, and the players rose early to pack the coach for their journey to Nîmes Airport. Emblazoned with a large official France 98 logo, the coach was unmistakable as the players squinted through the morning sun. Dressed in navy Umbro polo shirts and shorts to travel, the players mostly wore sunglasses to shield their eyes, and Brown's staff team were distinguishable by their blue navy Umbro tracksuit bottoms. Looking the part, the uniformity of Brown's regime now made perfect sense, and the squad did not look overwhelmed by the enormity of what lay ahead. Once in the coach, the steely professional ice was broken by the distribution of the players' photographic security passes, to be worn around their necks on lanyards. The players laughed hard at their photographs as they were passed around the coach, which alleviated some understandable nerves.

During the journey, pop music played in the background and, in *Craig Brown's World Cup Diary*, Christian Dailly turns to the camera in exasperation and enquires why they are not listening to credible bands like the Seahorses and Embrace. Dailly's 90s indie look is immediately identifiable, as he enquires why they are listening to the Spice Girls and Natalie Imbruglia. Most likely a generic album picked up at Glasgow Airport, Dailly clearly finds this chart pop excruciating, and is almost bent double. He then turns to Scot Gemmill, looking for the names of other artists he clearly dislikes. Gemmill helps his neighbour, suggesting All Saints. Dailly replies, 'Aye. All Saints. If this goes on any longer, I'm gonna have to take some drastic action!'

After disembarking at Nîmes Airport, the players unloaded their large personal Umbro sport bags, and the delegation then congregated in the departure lounge as they waited for their flight to Paris. Some players read newspapers, others cradled their mobile phones, which in 1998 were only useful for making calls and sending text messages. While waiting, masseur Stewart MacMillan confidently addressed the *World Cup Diary* camera. MacMillan savoured the occasion, saying that the players were ready for one of the biggest games in Scotland's history. MacMillan gauged the mood, adding that the players had had 'a right good laugh' the previous night. MacMillan looked around the departure lounge and commented that the players 'have all settled down, and it doesn't look as if there's any nerves around'. Dr John MacLean, Medical Officer, was next to address the *World Cup Diary* camera in equally confident mood, stating that the players were ready to be the best they could be. MacLean summed up the feelings of many Scots by describing the opportunity to play in the World Cup's opening match as a fantastic experience, with hopes of 'maybe even a wee result'.

Following their short flight, Scotland arrived in Paris to tight security. Another logoed France 98 coach was waiting to drive the delegation to their next destination of the day, the Stade de France, for a training session on the pitch. The players resumed reading newspapers, with card schools now developing on the coach tables. On arrival at Saint-Denis, the players understandably strained for their first view of the impressive Stade de France. When the structure first came into view against the bright Paris skyline, one player could be heard remarking on the *World Cup Diary*, 'A spaceship on tap ae it!'

The Scotland squad was greeted at the Stade de France by immaculate France 98 officials scurrying around, all with the aim of ensuring the smooth running of the tournament. With years of preparation now coming to fruition, Scotland were at the very centre of the activity, as they were chaperoned to their large changing room deep in the stadium. The players continued to look relaxed as they picked their changing room spots and slid their kit bags under the seated benches.

Craig Brown looked slightly more pensive as he made his way outside to survey the pitch. Standing, hand-on-hips, Brown assessed the chaotic scene. World Cup opening ceremony rehearsals were taking place, and Brown sought assurances from officials that his own schedule would not be affected before returning to the changing room to address his squad. Foremost in Brown's mind at this point was appeasing the media, and his *World Cup Diary* underlines how much this matter troubled him in contrast to the more straightforward task of training. Brown's players sat silently in the large changing room as he informed them of his dilemmas, greatest of which was the timing of that day's press conference at 4.30pm, which for Brown was a 'problem'. The players looked on with expressionless faces. They were by now kitted out in their white Umbro training tops and black shorts, in anticipation of their pitch training session, but Brown continued on the theme of briefing the press. His main concern was delaying the team announcement, and his solution was to make sure that the two players nominated to speak to the media did not give away the team selection, instead giving details to the Scottish dailies and not to the TV cameras. This way, the formal announcement would only appear in the following morning's papers.

With the players remaining seated and silent, Brown did then outline his plans for the day's training session. Brown was noticeably more relaxed following the change of subject, alleviating the slight tension in the changing room atmosphere. Brown referred to his white board tactics sheets, which divided the squad into three groups, with Paul Lambert nominated as a floater between groups. The hamper boys were also included in the training drills. Brown stated that the squad would warm up together, do a bit of pairs work with the ball on the ground, then the passing exercise they had done the previous day, followed by just 'playing the usual'. Brown added that they would be 'kidding them on a bit [Brazil via the observing media]'. The plan was to 'stick out a back four, with two strikers' and 'play the six against the four'. Then they would 'go in' with 'eight against four, so the attacks should be good'. Lambert was of course the floater across the groups, so it would be nine against four. This would mean 'attack, go out again, attack, out again'.

Out on the pitch, the players jogged around in the impressive surroundings, as physiotherapist Pip Yeates led the warm-up. The goalkeepers warmed up separately, and livewire Jonathan Gould addressed the *World Cup Diary*, quipping that it was, 'nearly as impressive as Celtic Park. But not quite.'

The main objective of the session was for the players to get a feel for the speed of the ball over the playing surface, and Brown highlighted that motivation certainly was not a problem on the day, as the players completed familiar training exercises in the magnificent purpose-built arena. With Alex Miller directing the session, Craig Brown found the opportunity to address his video diary directly and recounted his previous experiences of the spectacular venue. Brown, as previously mentioned, had been at the stadium's opening match on 28 January 1998, a 1–0 friendly victory for France versus Spain, in bitterly cold temperatures, when the 'pitch was frozen'. Brown had also attended a 'workshop for coaches', where the pitch had still been 'bumpy', and had met Mário Zagallo, Brazil's head coach, and 'had a walk across the pitch and a chat'. 'But as you can see now, the place is magnificent,' Brown told the *World Cup Diary*, 'and the players are looking very healthy. They are looking well. They are ready for the match tomorrow, and they are looking forward to it.'

The focus in the Stade de France then turned to one unfortunate player sitting on the sidelines, Gary McAllister. Sitting in a dugout looking on, McAllister was distinguishable from the rest of the squad in his navy travelling attire and sunglasses. McAllister sat drinking from a large bottle of water as he was approached by the video diary, and was asked for his opinion on Scotland's chances against Brazil. McAllister replied, 'I fancy us tomorrow. Yeah. A wee upset and an open game. That would be nice.' McAllister, well accustomed to TV interviews as Scotland's usual captain, seemed slightly uncertain when approached in this informal manner. His evaluation of Scotland's chances was nonetheless sincere.

Following their training session, the Scotland squad and delegation were then taken by coach to their five-star château hotel 40km away in the beautiful location of Chantilly, on the outskirts of Paris. The players relaxed on the balconies in their shorts and shades, as the blazered SFA officials and members of the international committee milled around in the background. The well-mannered Craig Brown, with his vast experience as both a teaching professional and ex-professional footballer, was the perfect go-between to bridge the two worlds. With the match of their lives now only 24 hours away, it felt like the gaze of the entire planet had now fallen upon Brown and his players.

The late-afternoon atmosphere and level of security at the hotel were already unique in the history of the Scotland National Team, and UK Prime Minister Tony Blair had now arrived to meet the squad and wish them luck. Blair saw football as very compatible with his 'Cool Britannia' image, and with the arrival of all-seater stadia, football was now no longer the sport of hooligans in designer sportswear locked inside cages. English football in the 1990s had been cleaned up and rebranded as the Premier League, and Blair had therefore sought to capitalise with an expensive power-play for England to host the World Cup in 2006. Though Blair was Edinburgh-born and had also lived in Glasgow during his childhood, the nation of Scotland does not appear to have been part of his football masterplan, though the eventual awarding of the 2006 tournament to Germany renders this point academic.

However, drawing again from the *World Cup Diary*, on 9 June 1998, Tony Blair, wearing an impeccable navy-blue suit and tie, was in full flight as he was shepherded towards the château balcony to meet the waiting Scotland players by his security detail and Vice-President of the SFA John McBeth. Blair then emerged into the bright afternoon sunshine. The players reacted with a hesitant impromptu round of applause and uncertainty at what they should do next. Blair addressed the group immediately, stating, 'Our hopes are with you tomorrow. The whole country is behind you.' Typically of a UK Prime Minister, Blair used the word 'country' to define a union of four nations, two of which were competing at the same World Cup finals. After unconsciously reducing the nation of Scotland to a region with his opening sentence, Blair did then looked genuinely moved as he addressed the players again and said, 'I can't imagine what it must be like for you guys. It is just the most fantastic thing in the world.'

Blair beamed, and then Craig Brown began introducing the players and staff one by one. Blair seemed to know English football fairly well, possibly surprising the players as he first chatted to captain Colin Hendry and then to Gordon Durie about his spells with Chelsea and Tottenham Hotspur. A player's voice could then be heard interjecting at the perfect moment, to suggest Tottenham were a better team since Durie had left! All the players laughed, reducing the tension. Next, Blair stopped at Paul Lambert, and told him that he had read an excellent story about him in the *Observer* newspaper about his time with Borussia Dortmund. Lambert acknowledged this, looking slightly unsure how best to accept the Prime Minister's compliments. Brown then moved to John Collins, mentioning that Collins was able to speak French, which impressed Blair, who had spent time in France after obtaining his law degree but had not learned the language. Of all the players, Collins was the most confident in the Prime Minister's presence, striking up a good rapport. Blair's last main stop was with Colin Calderwood, with whom he chatted about Tottenham Hotspur – before identifying himself as a Newcastle United supporter, which he truly was, having also spent his later childhood in the north-east of England.

At the conclusion of the introductions, Hendry, Collins and Gallacher presented Blair with numbered Scotland home shirts, and Jim McBeth gave a short speech thanking the Prime Minister for his visit. At the end of a long and exhausting day for the players, a dinner buffet was served inside the hotel, with Blair providing photo opportunities for the SFA international committee. On the *World Cup Diary*, Collins can again be seen chatting to the Prime Minister – maybe Collins was considering a career in politics after retirement! But there were more important matters at hand for now, and the big day had almost arrived.

9
BRAZIL

Wednesday 10 June 1998 was a pleasant day in Chantilly, and Scotland's players enjoyed a carbohydrate-loaded meal in the morning in the grand dining room of the château hotel. A journey which had begun on a cold night in Vienna on 31 August 1996 had now culminated in preparations for the biggest match in the history of the Scotland National Team.

After their meal, the players were offered a massage in a customised hotel suite containing portable massage tables. The *World Cup Diary* shows masseur Stewart MacMillan joking with captain Colin Hendry, who is receiving a massage from Pip Yeates. MacMillan initially places a pair of underpants on his head. In response, a stone-faced Hendry looks at MacMillan, and applying his dry sense of humour tells the camera he wore the underpants at yesterday's training session. MacMillan sheepishly takes the pants off his head.

Kevin Gallacher compared the atmosphere in the hotel that morning to attending a wedding. His team-mates all seemed to agree with this remark, perhaps owing to their opportunity to wear the full national dress. The squad's decision to wear kilts to the Stade de France had been a closely-kept secret, and almost 23 years later, when talking to the *Official Scotland Podcast*, Gallacher and Hendry remembered the experience vividly. 'I remember we had the meeting,' said Gallacher. 'We all went, "Yes, we're all up for the kilt, no other national team has done it. Let's go and enjoy it. Let's go and do something for the nation and make them proud of us." We couldn't tell anybody! We told the wives, "You can't tell anybody!"' Hendry remembered the experience equally fondly. 'It was a one-off,' Hendry said, "really, really special. Everybody was really, really into it. It was important at that point of time that you were Scottish, even if you were born in England. Even if you were there because your grandad's Scottish, your dad's Scottish, your mum... You're Scottish. You're playing for Scotland. You've been picked to play for Scotland, and that's it. That was the focal point of it all.'

Prior to departing on the 40km coach journey to Saint-Denis, Craig Brown encouraged the players to take one last chance to relax, which they gratefully accepted by taking a stroll around the picturesque grounds of the château.

While the players were on their walk, physiotherapist Hugh Allan, incredibly now at his eighth major tournament with Scotland, shared a few words with the *World Cup Diary*. Allan was clearly more worried about his role as kit man than physio. 'If there's one thing out, I'm in bother,' Allan commented. 'Everything's got to be bang in order. So, I won't be happy until everybody's stripped, and nobody's shouting for something they haven't got. So hopefully, we're there.' The veteran, who had seen it all before, and knew exactly what to expect, then put his thumbs up to the camera. On his eventual retirement, in a career spanning around 270 internationals under six Scotland managers, Allan had served Scotland's National Team at six World Cups and two European Championships. It is unlikely that we will see his like again.

The first official photographs of Scotland's squad and backroom staff wearing the aptly named National Tartan, which was mainly navy in colour with a fine red stripe, were taken at the front of their waiting France 98 logoed coach. Due to the heat, the players had removed their jackets, and wore white dress shirts and dark ties for the journey. As with previous coach journeys, most wore shades due to the bright French sun, and the card schools started immediately after the players were seated.

During the 40-minute journey, as the players tried to relax by listening to music, Brown addressed his *World Cup Diary* directly. Scotland's official World Cup track, recorded by Scottish rock band Del Amitri, could be heard in the background, as Brown read out good luck faxes sent by well-wishers such as the Scotland National Rugby Team, Gordon Strachan and golfer Colin Montgomerie. Brown also remarked that iconic Scottish actor Sean Connery was in Paris and expected at the match. On the subject of the kilts, Brown was by now as enthused as his players, stating, 'If that gives us a bit of inspiration, you never know.' It seemed the ever-meticulous Brown had by now evaluated that his squad's immense pride in their appearance might just provide an 'aggregate marginal gain'.

Scotland's delegation arrived at the Stade de France at 3.30pm, two hours before kick-off. As the coach picked its way slowly through the crowds, the players could not contain themselves, and crowded at the coach windows, where they were able to engage temporarily with the carnival atmosphere outside. In a sea of colour, kilted members of the Tartan Army in replica shirts mixed with face-painted Brazilians with drums and horns. Handshakes and embraces were exchanged as two football-obsessed cultures merged. Flags bearing the St Andrew's cross were interspersed with brilliant Brazilian yellow and green, as fans from both nations drank lager from plastic cups and ate lunch together at food stalls. The Tartan Army had arrived early, and thousands were already inside the cavernous stadium.

As the players disembarked the coach from the enclosed parking area in the Stade de France, the world caught their first glimpse of Scotland in their kilt uniform. On arrival the players first carried their large numbered Umbro kit bags to their dressing room, a familiar environment due to the previous day's training session. Next, the players were led along the tunnel towards the pitch by their appointed FIFA liaison officer. As usual, captain Colin Hendry was first to emerge into the bright Paris sunshine. The noise of a rhythmic instrumental drum track was being pumped around the stadium by huge speakers. Thousands were already inside, many of whom were dancing and swaying to the music, waving their drinks to the camera as they partied.

It took a moment or two before the Tartan Army realised that the players had arrived on the pitch, and it was the tracksuited Brazilian backroom staff who noticed Scotland first. Standing at pitchside in their oversized sports garments, the Brazilian delegation stood staring as Craig Brown's kilted men swaggered confidently onto the Stade de France turf. A moment later, the Tartan Army realised their heroes had arrived, and an enormous cheer echoed around the arena. The players instinctively raised their arms aloft in unison and began applauding above their heads. Kilted backroom staff Alan Hodgkinson, Stewart MacMillan, Hugh Allan, team doctor Stewart Hillis and Pip Yeates also strode proudly onto the turf, with Craig Brown and Alex Miller having opted instead for smart navy-blue suits with an embroidered yellow crest badge. The clothing choice of Brown and Miller set them apart from the rest of the delegation, which struck a slightly authoritarian tone and fitted the scene perfectly.

Hendry was filmed greeting and embracing his family in the stands, as photographers in red France 98 logoed vests crowded around Hendry to obtain some of the earliest tournament photographs. Television camera operators, distinguishable in their blue vests, filmed Scotland's spectacular arrival. Hypervigilant stewards, seeking to avoid any last-minute mishaps following years of careful preparation, scuttled around to ensure the safety of the players and the smooth running of proceedings.

Following the emotional pitch scene, the players returned to their changing room for FIFA to check the players' accreditation, contained within the lanyards worn around their necks. Everyone was present and correct as the crisp navy Umbro Scotland home shirts with bright white numbers and lettering were handed out. Most players were by now wearing their officially-numbered match shorts, but left their match shirts to one side in preference of white Umbro training tops for the warm-up.

Craig Brown's perfectly co-ordinated match preparations were significantly disrupted at this point, however. They had been informed only the previous day that, due to the World Cup's opening ceremony taking priority, they would be unable to conduct their warm-up routines on the

Stade de France pitch. Speaking on the *Official Scotland Podcast*, Kevin Gallacher recalled the psychological impact of this disruption. 'It was unbelievable,' Gallacher said. 'We're gonna go out, we'll warm up as normal... No. You've got a room, 20 ft by 20 ft, with a pillar in the middle. I think we struggled to come to terms with that mentally. It was like someone just painting over a window. We couldn't see out.'

In their trainers, training tops and match shorts, the players therefore adapted as best they could to these unanticipated circumstances. Although FIFA had declared that the area was a 'custom-designed warm-up room', Gallacher's analysis was more accurate. The crowded players stretched and attempted ball work within the confined space, grappling with the inconvenient pillar, and being forced to run up and down corridors to loosen up. The chaotic scene included a goalkeeping warm-up, with Hodgkinson firing shots across the room into the arms of Jim Leighton. Jackie McNamara stood doing keepy-ups in a corner, while others ran through a variety of stretches wherever they could find space. It was far from an ideal preparation for the biggest match of their lives, but as Gallacher also acknowledged, both teams were impacted equally by these unforeseen circumstances.

At 5pm, 30 minutes before kick-off, the players were mostly seated again and taking on fluids. Hendry was handed the navy and yellow embroidered SFA match pennant to exchange with Brazilian captain Dunga. Alex Miller's voice could be heard above the rest, as his many years of managerial experience came to the fore. The *World Cup Diary* captured the frenetic scene, with Miller addressing the dressing room loudly with positive imperatives like, 'Let's test the goalie,' 'Let's test the defenders,'

'Let's have a go at them,' and 'Try and achieve getting the ball in their box early doors.'

The players responded to Miller's motivational words with shouts of, 'C'mon lads!' With the big moment looming, the players exchanged customary handshakes and embraces in the dressing room. Colin Calderwood, stripped to the waist, was a picture of intensity. His eyes bulged from his head as he gritted his teeth and puffed out his cheeks. Calderwood shouted, 'C'mon boys. Let's get out there and give it a go!' Others immediately joined in with Calderwood, shouting, 'Let's stick together, boys.' Then, suddenly, Hendry was standing at the dressing room door, ball in hand. Hendry rapped on the doorframe, and gave the battle cry, shouting above all others, 'C'mon lads. Let's go, eh? C'mon!'

Hendry then turned on his heels and strode confidently towards the pitch, never looking back. Scotland's spectacular reward for two years of resilience and professionalism had now come to fruition. Scotland's players observed their superstitions as they trooped out behind Hendry one by one. For example, John Collins remained stripped to the waist until the very last possible moment, and Darren Jackson insisted on being last to leave the changing room. Calderwood, now like a wild man, emerged just before Jackson, slapping his bare chest and shouting, 'C'mon!' at the top of his voice. In a frenzy, Calderwood turned right as he left the changing room, rather than left towards the pitch, raising a smile from Jackson, who had conversely prepared himself by remaining completely relaxed. Calderwood was shepherded towards the pitch by bewildered FIFA stadium delegates, as the ice-cool Jackson waited for his confused team-mate to become properly orientated.

As for Scotland's fearsome opponents, following a shock 1–0 defeat at the Maracanã to arch-rivals Argentina in April 1998, Brazil's head coach Mário Zagallo had taken the unprecedented step of naming his final 22-man squad, and his team to face Scotland in the opening match, over four weeks earlier. A World Cup winner as a player in 1958 and 1962, and as head coach and assistant coach in 1970 and 1994 respectively, Zagallo had been involved in four previous World Cup victories. No other Brazilian could match Zagallo's World Cup record, though the Brazilian public had recently grown impatient with his team's mediocre performances and results.

Having qualified automatically for France 98 as holders, Brazil's World Cup preparations had been disrupted by so-called 'Nike friendlies', which *World Soccer* defined as Brazil accepting sponsor-led matches anywhere and at any time, irrespective of which players were available. Consequently, during his four years in charge, Zagallo had been forced to field over 100 different players, and Brazil were widely criticised for a lack of on-field cohesion and understanding following the Argentina defeat. To rub salt in the wounds, Argentina head coach and pantomime villain Daniel Passarella had been on-hand to call Brazil 'predictable', leading to a classic Brazilian crisis of confidence on the eve of the tournament.

Possibly pre-empting these difficulties, and with the aim of improving Brazil's attacking prowess, the CBF had appointed ex-star player Zico as Zagallo's assistant in March 1998. As a player, Zico had won 71 caps for Brazil, scoring an impressive 48 international goals, and speculation abounded that the maverick move of announcing Brazil's team so early was also Zico's idea. In any case, the distraction had the desired effect, and Brazil's attacking line-up named to face Scotland temporarily appeased the football-obsessed Brazilian public.

The main talking point arising from Brazil's early team announcement was the omission of the world's most expensive player, 20-year-old Denílson, who had recently confirmed a £21.5-million move from São Paulo to Real Betis. Like so many young Brazilian stars, Denílson was already battle-hardened, having played an incredible 198 matches for São Paulo prior to moving to La Liga, despite his tender age.

Although named in the original first eleven to face Scotland, the fitness of 1994 World Cup hero Romário was also a major talking point during Brazil's preparations. The talented striker had been struggling for some time with an injury to his right calf, and by early June it had become apparent that the diminutive striker was not fit enough for inclusion. At the corresponding press conference to announce his withdrawal, in a dramatic display of public emotion, Romário covered his face with his hands as he broke down and choked back the tears. Romário's place in Brazil's team to face Scotland was taken by Bebeto, his strike partner from the 1994 World Cup, and his squad place was, rather surprisingly, handed to defensive midfielder Emerson, as opposed to another striker.

Overall, however, despite their recent performance stutters, and the expected off-field drama, Brazil had an abundance of talent in their squad, and were clear favourites to win the tournament.

Meanwhile, outside in the gleaming Stade de France, the atmosphere was at fever pitch. A typical opening ceremony featured the usual colourful choreographed displays involving hundreds of dancers. Three thousand balloons were released into the Paris sky, and huge inflatable flowers opened to reveal trampolinists. Costumed stilt-walkers paraded the pitch as enormous footballs were released from centrepiece displays. Theme music blared as coloured smoke poured from smoke machines.

When the choreography had concluded, the big moment arrived. Scotland and Brazil emerged from the Stade de France tunnel at the same moment, either side of the red-shirted referee José Maria García-Aranda of Spain, and his assistant referees Fernando Tresaco Gracia, also of Spain, and Jorge Luis Arango of Colombia. Scotland, led by talisman Colin Hendry, marched into the cauldron of energy with looks of steely determination etched on their faces. Contrastingly, Brazil filtered onto the pitch hand-in-hand, led by captain Dunga, the little metronomic midfielder who had held the World Cup aloft four years earlier in the Rose Bowl, Pasadena.

Prior to the national anthems, quiet was requested in the stadium to observe a speech from exiting FIFA President João Havelange. In a moment typical of the Tartan Army, choruses of boos, whistles and songs suddenly erupted within their ranks, ensuring Havelange's speech was drowned out entirely in their section of the stadium. Following a rousing rendition of 'Flower of Scotland', during which all Scotland's players sang, Hendry observed the coin toss, and at 5.30pm, kick-off time had arrived.

I detailed how Scotland were to line up in their 3–5–2 formation in the previous chapter, but now let's run the rule over Mário Zagallo's side facing them in a 4–4–2 formation on this momentous evening.

In order of squad numbers, the Brazil team were as follows: Taffarel (1); Cafu (2); Aldair (3); Júnior Baiano (4); César Sampaio (5); Roberto Carlos (6); Giovanni (7); Dunga (8); Ronaldo (9); Rivaldo (10); Bebeto (20).

First Half

Scotland kicked off to rapturous cheering and applause, and the Tartan Army greeted each pass with '*Olé!*' as Scotland knocked the ball around. A loud boo then rang out as Brazil gained possession for the first time. Alarmingly, Ronaldo showed his strength and balance immediately, shrugging off a stern but fair challenge from Colin Calderwood and passing to Roberto Carlos, who had popped up deep inside Scotland's half. Brazil's number ten, Rivaldo, then suddenly ghosted into space to collect the ball from the feet of Carlos. Scotland's energetic pressing then broke up this promising first-minute move, with Gordon Durie seeing the ball safely out of play for a goal kick.

The goal kick was taken short by Jim Leighton, with Paul Lambert immediately offering a passing outlet for the three centre-backs: Calderwood (right centre-back), Colin Hendry (centre-back) and Tom Boyd (left centre-back). However, Lambert uncharacteristically gave the ball away cheaply in midfield, and the move broke down almost immediately. For a split second, it looked as if Ronaldo might have something to work with, but he was pressed by Scotland's back line, and the ball ran harmlessly back to goalkeeper Leighton.

Next Leighton tried his first long goal kick of the afternoon, with the ball reaching Brazil's right-back Cafu, who collected and attempted to play out of defence. Encouragingly, Scotland's attacking press smothered Cafu, and the ball broke dangerously to Durie in the Brazilian box. It looked momentarily as if Durie was bowled over by Brazil's right centre-back Júnior Baiano, but there was no appeal from Durie as he rose to his feet.

This time, Brazil opted to kick long from defence, and Hendry collected the ball at the opposite end of the pitch and fed Boyd, who was hugging the touchline in Scotland's left-back position. Christian Dailly, Scotland's left wing-back, had taken up a more advanced position on the left, applying Craig Brown's instructions to restrict Cafu's space. Boyd chose to play a long diagonal ball out of defence, which Baiano collected once more for Brazil.

This time the Brazilians were less wasteful playing out from defence, and Bebeto was able to collect the ball in an advanced position and link with the elusive Rivaldo, who was able to skip away from the attentions of Lambert with a change of pace that brought roars of appreciation from the Stade de France crowd. Rivaldo then fed central defensive midfielder Dunga, who was supporting the attack. Dunga gathered the ball and hit a speculative long-range shot on goal which Hendry headed as he was moving to his left, causing the ball to drift past Leighton's right-hand post, providing Brazil with a relatively cheap early corner kick.

Bebeto sauntered out to take the corner from Brazil's left-hand side of the pitch, and shaped up for a right-footed inswinger. The little striker's timing appeared to catch Scotland napping, and his corner kick looped towards the front post, with Scotland's defence caught on their heels. Unfortunately for Scotland, Brazilian midfielder César Sampaio was the player most switched on in the penalty area, and he attacked Bebeto's corner at Scotland's near post. Sampaio beat his marker Craig Burley to the ball, glancing a header powerfully and accurately goalwards. John Collins moved off Scotland's right-hand post in a last-ditch effort to salvage the situation, but sank to his knees as the ball hit the back of Leighton's net. Sampaio reeled away in celebration and dropped to his knees as he was mobbed by his ecstatic teammates. A goal for Brazil after just four minutes, and the worst possible start for Scotland.

In the *Official Scotland Podcast*, Kevin Gallacher has linked this defensive error and uncharacteristically sloppy early goal with Scotland's disrupted warm-up preparations. 'We never let teams score from set pieces,' Gallacher added. 'In the whole campaign, I think we must have let in one set piece. 'But yet, in the opening 15 minutes, we switched off.'

Encouragingly, Scotland's body language did not alter as they jogged into position for the restart. The ball was immediately fed out to Boyd from the centre circle, but Boyd opted to play a long diagonal ball once more, giving up possession to a Brazilian team in the ascendancy. Brazil began to stroke the ball around confidently, but were unable to find any rhythm, allowing Scotland to break up their move fairly easily. Scotland aimed long again, with Durie the target this time, but once again they gave the ball away.

This time Brazil chose to play out of defence, possibly feeling they already had Scotland on the ropes due to the early sucker-punch goal. Dunga collected the ball from his defence and played an accurate searching ball towards Rivaldo, who was bounding forwards once more. Lambert had tracked Rivaldo's run, restricting his space, but the talented left-footed midfielder was able to play a dangerous ball into Scotland's box, which was well watched by Hendry, who headed out of play for another Brazilian corner. Once again, Bebeto trotted out to take the kick, and swung in a similar right-footed cross. But this time Scotland were alive to the situation, and the ball was headed clear.

In the next passage of play, referee José Maria García-Aranda was required to make a decision for the first time as the competitive Durie arrived late in a challenge on Baiano. The Brazilian players pleaded with García-Aranda to punish Durie with a card, but encouragingly the Spanish referee waved them away with an air of authority. This boded well, indicating that the official was not 'card-happy' or overwhelmed by refereeing this momentous occasion.

In the exchanges that followed, Brazil tried to assert their authority by building the play from the back through Dunga. However, the harrying press of Gallacher was becoming increasingly effective as the forward worked himself into the match. The eager running of Durie and Jackson complemented Gallacher's energetic press, and Brazil were not able to dominate Scotland in the manner they perhaps anticipated, despite their one-goal advantage. Correspondingly, John Collins began to find pockets of space in the midfield as Scotland began to settle into the match.

Scotland's competitive edge soon won them their first corner, and Collins was given a hero's reception as he jogged out to take the kick directly under the Tartan Army. Big men Hendry and Calderwood advanced, expecting a left footed inswinger from set-piece specialist Collins. Surprisingly, Collins did not clear the first man with his corner, allowing midfielder Giovanni to head to relative safety. Scotland continued to exert pressure via a long throw-in attempt from Durie, but this time Carlos cleared after Brazil again won the aerial exchange. Burley attempted a second throw-in, but Jackson was penalised for a flailing arm which caught Carlos.

This action took place on Scotland's right, with considerable pressure exerted on Brazil's left-back Carlos. On Scotland's left, Dailly was stifling Cafu as instructed, and Brazil were having difficulty coming to terms with Scotland's hard running and neat interplay. Dunga must have observed Cafu's quiet start to the match, as the next time he received the ball he fired a long diagonal pass into Brazil's right-wing area. Cafu had sprinted the length of the pitch in an effort to get himself into the game, but cut a frustrated figure when the ball rolled out of play just beyond his reach.

Leighton went long again from the resulting goal kick, which Brazil returned with more purpose this time. Again, Dunga was involved as he fed Rivaldo in the central attacking-midfield position. This time, Rivaldo tried his luck with a left-footed shot from just outside Scotland's penalty area, which Leighton easily saved, before throwing the ball quickly to Burley in the right-back position. Burley laid the ball off to Calderwood, but another long, misplaced diagonal ball out of defence again wasted possession for Scotland.

Dunga collected the ball and played yet another awkward looping pass, which bounced dangerously in Scotland's box, splitting the on-rushing Leighton and back-pedalling Hendry. With limited options available to him, Hendry completed a firm flying header as Ronaldo tracked the loose ball, looking sure to pounce on any hesitation. The header beat Leighton, and for a moment it looked like a spectacular own goal. Fortunately for Scotland, the ball trundled past Leighton's left-hand post to safety.

Scotland cleared the resulting corner, and the next few exchanges of play were scrappy as both teams attempted overly-ambitious passes out of defence. Lambert cleverly began to address this by dropping deep to link Scotland's defence and midfield, and in doing so was able to create neat triangles of play with Collins and Burley. However, the intelligence of Carlos was a constant thorn in Burley's side, as the little Brazilian seemed to pop up from nowhere on Brazil's left whenever adventurous wing-back Burley attempted to support Scotland's attack.

The next passages of play saw Jackson more involved in his deeper-than-usual right central-midfield position. Jackson was far from intimidated by the reputation of the Brazilians, and appeared intent on ruffling their feathers at every available opportunity.

Then came the moment that Craig Brown had dreaded. Dailly made his first attempt to break forwards from his left wing-back position, but Cafu ruthlessly exploited the space left in behind Dailly after the move broke down. Ronaldo had also read the situation and immediately got ready to receive the ball from his favourite supplier. With long elegant strides, blistering pace and mesmerising ball control, Ronaldo demonstrated for the first time in the match why he was considered the world's best player. With his trademark movement, Ronaldo drew in both Hendry and Boyd on Brazil's right wing. Seemingly going nowhere, Ronaldo suddenly turned and checked back inside, using his bodyweight to ride Boyd's challenge and propel himself into Scotland's penalty area. From one moment to the next, Hendry and Boyd were completely beaten, and Ronaldo unleashed a powerful right-footed shot towards the left corner of the net. In an instant, Leighton dived down to his right, making an incredible one-handed reflex save of supreme quality. In a heartbeat, 39-year-old Leighton had demonstrated why he would come to be considered one of Scotland's greatest-ever international players.

In the subsequent exchanges of play, Scotland began to gain a firmer foothold in the match, with Lambert continually collecting the ball out of defence, allowing neat triangles of play to develop between the busy Scotland midfield and forward line. It was clear by now that Brazil's centre-backs, Aldair and Baiano, were not enjoying playing against Durie and Gallacher. Correspondingly, the more Brazil's defensive players were occupied by Scotland's two forwards, the more Collins was able to craft and create from midfield. Jackson, however, went too far with his efforts to disrupt Brazil's flow, and received the tournament's first yellow card for a late challenge on Dunga.

Then, a big chance for Scotland. Hendry, who had become increasingly commanding at the back as the first half progressed, won a long clearance from Brazilian goalkeeper Taffarel in the air. Jackson collected the loose ball and played a sharp pass along Scotland's right wing towards Gallacher, who reached the ball at Brazil's byline ahead of Dunga. Gallacher was then able to hook a dangerous right-footed cross into the penalty area, which had the Brazil defence back-pedalling. Durie had matched Gallacher's run, and the cross looked absolutely perfect for Durie to meet with his head from six yards out. As Durie stooped to head the ball, neck muscles flexed and ready, Baiano produced one of the most spectacular defensive clearances you are ever likely to see, flying through the air and catching the ball with his heel for a scorpion-kick volley, the ball sailing out of play to safety. Taffarel stood over the big defender and applauded this incredible play, while Durie looked absolutely mystified as to why the ball had not reached his head!

But this at least showed that Scotland were very much in

the match, and as half time approached, they received the reward their resilience and good play deserved. On 35 minutes, Lambert collected the ball from Calderwood deep inside Scotland's half and moved up the pitch, linking with Jackson, who made further progress into Brazilian territory. Jackson was closed down but rode the challenge, and retained possession for Gallacher, who was in support. Gallacher kept up momentum by knocking the ball back to Burley, who was supporting the attack from his right wing-back position. Gallacher then turned on his heels and darted towards the Brazilian box, leaving Burley to play a perfect long diagonal ball into the Brazilian box, aimed at Durie and Dailly, who had supported the attack from Scotland's left. Dailly, who had been restricted mostly to defensive duties in the first half, was suddenly an unexpected attacking presence, leaving Baiano exposed in a two-on-one. Durie, as usual, contested the ball with maximum effort, and Baiano could not deal with both Scotland players. Dailly rose highest in the Brazilian box and headed towards the irrepressible Gallacher, who had continued his run, and was by now in behind Brazil's back line. Sampaio had tracked Gallacher's run, but was on the wrong side of Gallacher, causing him to collide clumsily with the Scotland forward. Gallacher crumpled to the turf on contact, and the referee had no hesitation in pointing to the spot for a penalty kick. Sampaio stood, hands-on-hips, looking disconsolate as he was issued with a yellow card. Taffarel charged towards the referee, waving his finger in protest. The referee waved away the Brazilian appeals and Scotland had a well-deserved route back into the match.

Clearly, Taffarel felt that Gallacher had made the most of the contact to win the spot kick, but Gallacher was clear about what happened when he later described the penalty incident on the *Official Scotland Podcast*. 'I didn't really dive in my career, but against Sweden in Sweden [in France 98 qualification], I had a very similar opportunity,' said Gallacher, 'and I stood up, thinking, "I can maybe get the ball and try and score here." It didn't happen, and it was an opportunity wasted really, and that stuck in my head.' Back at the Stade de France, Gallacher had felt that Taffarel was going to beat him to the ball, but, 'All of a sudden, I just felt the hands on my back,' said Gallacher. 'I didn't dive, I just fell over, and as I fell over, basically... the noise – I just thought, was that the whistle?' The referee was indeed pointing at the spot. Next on Gallacher's mind was who would be brave enough to take advantage and try to beat Taffarel, but he need not have worried. 'I looked around, and John Collins had the ball, peacocking, confident, and he just walked away,' adds Gallacher. 'And I thought, "Thank God somebody's confident about taking the penalty!"'

Collins, Scotland's cultured left-footed midfielder, now had the eyes of billions concentrating on his next kick of a football. As Collins placed the Adidas Tricolore ball, with its distinctive Tango design, on the penalty spot, current holder of the Ballon d'Or Ronaldo continued to remonstrate with the referee in the background. Never before or since has a Scottish footballer had so much pressure on his shoulders. Collins stood, hands-on-hips, breathing deeply and looking down at the ball. The referee eventually cleared the penalty area, jogged backwards, stood in position and blew his whistle, granting Collins permission to take the kick. Collins wasted little time, shaping his run and puffing his cheeks out as he connected perfectly with the ball with the side of his left foot. Taffarel, who had been jumping back and forth on the goal line attempting to unsettle Collins, dived desperately down to his right, the correct direction. But Collins knew immediately that he had scored and reeled away in jubilation, sprinting towards the Tartan Army as the ball nestled in the back of the Brazilian net. The Scottish section of the Stade de France absolutely erupted as the travelling fans roared with delight and dived all over each other, barely believing Scotland had drawn level with the world champions in the World Cup's opening match. Collins' years of professionalism and dedication had been rewarded in the most spectacular of circumstances, as he planted his feet in front of the Tartan Army, back turned, and pointed to the name across the back of his shirt. Perhaps never has a goal been celebrated so intensely in Scotland. It was the 38th minute of a pulsating half and the score was 1–1.

The remainder of the first half flew past in something of a blur, as the shell-shocked Brazilians mainly tried, unsuccessfully, to reassert themselves against a combative Scotland team in the ascendancy. On 44 minutes, Brazilian head coach Zagallo was suddenly seen at the touchline, shouting angrily at his players. The equaliser looked like perfect revenge for Craig Brown's men after a leaked story in the preceding days claimed that Zagallo had allegedly made scathing remarks about Scotland's chances in the match. Although the rumours were unproven, it's likely that the sight of Brazil's most successful World Cup figure looking bitter and animated on the touchline did Scotland's morale no harm at all.

Half Time

The dressing-room scene at half time is captured on the *World Cup Diary*, with Craig Brown addressing his players and congratulating them on a 'magnificent' second 25 minutes of the half but also scolding them, saying, 'We always have to claw our way back from a goal behind. Why do we have to do that?' For the second half, Brown encouraged his players to play the early ball to try to grab a second goal by getting 'balls quickly up to the front, and then out to the channels'. He reminded them that the Brazilian back line had struggled every time Gordon Durie or Kevin Gallacher had picked up the ball. Brown then again praised his side's 'brilliant character, coming back after losing a goal so early.'

Watching the scene back in the *World Cup Diary*, the team look relatively calm. Craig Burley is leaning forwards, listening intently. Christian Dailly, perhaps the player with the toughest brief, of marking Cafu to prevent Ronaldo receiving the pass, nods in agreement when Brown addresses him directly. Colin Hendry and Paul Lambert sit next to each other, taking on fluids and listening. The two front men, Durie and Gallacher, are stripped to the waist, trying to cool off, after an incredible running shift in the opening 45 minutes. Colin Calderwood still looks a pumped-up figure as he receives attention from physio Hugh Allan in the background. By contrast, Jackson sits calmly, arms folded, appearing unruffled. Tom Boyd presents as somewhere in between, stripped to the waist, with one leg on a bench in a relaxed position. Brown and Alex Miller prowl up and down the dressing room like the perfect double-act. When Brown finishes speaking, Miller immediately addresses the players, seamlessly following Brown's words, telling them that they might have been 'a wee bit nervy at the start' but that they had got over this. 'We don't want to be brave losers,' Miller adds. John Collins then erupts, understandably inspired and pumping with adrenaline after his goal, shouting, 'Hey. Confidence.

C'mon! We're gonna win.' Then other players join in with Collins: 'C'mon! Believe.'

Second Half

Prior to the restart, the referee requested additional pegs be added to Jim Leighton's net, sending the FIFA stadium delegates scampering around once more. Once resolved, Brazil kicked off, and Cafu chipped a ball down their right wing. Leonardo, who had been introduced as a half-time substitute for Giovanni, chased down the ball. The surprise of facing a new player of this stature appeared to catch Scotland slightly off-guard, and following a tackle on Leonardo from Tom Boyd, Brazil won a corner. Leonardo immediately placed the ball by the corner flag in front of the Tartan Army, and swung in a left-footed ball, which did not clear the first man, Darren Jackson, who headed out of play for another corner. Again, Leonardo's left-footed attempt was headed clear, but this time only as far as Cafu, who unleashed a powerful shot on goal. Gordon Durie bravely stood up to the ball, which caught him square in the face and bounced to eventual safety. Durie lay sprawled on the turf, requiring a stoppage, and Scotland were given a temporary reprieve.

In the next passage of play, a superb dummy from Ronaldo wrong-footed Colin Calderwood and freed Rivaldo in a central attacking position. In his elusive style, Rivaldo chopped one way and then the other, outfoxing his marker Paul Lambert. Rivaldo then unleashed a ferocious left-footed, low-driven shot, which arrowed past Leighton's right post. Brazil seemed in the mood, but were broken up by a roving run from Christian Dailly, who had followed Craig Brown's half-time advice to get forward more often. The move broke down, but Scotland had at least now gained a foothold in the second period.

Rivaldo again tried to assert himself in the match, carrying the ball forwards and feeding Bebeto, who had had a relatively quiet match as Brazil's second striker. A superb sliding tackle from Lambert robbed Bebeto and carried the ball in the opposite direction. Lambert then fed Gallacher, who got another good cross into the opposing penalty area, which was well watched by the Brazilian defence.

Moments later, Jackson broke up a Brazilian move and carried the ball upfield, feeding Kevin Gallacher, who was now causing more problems for Brazil with his running in the channels. This led to a tame shot by Dailly, easily saved by Taffarel. Brazil then moved the ball upfield quickly themselves, leading to another venomous left-footed Rivaldo strike from a least 30 yards out that rose only marginally too high and wide.

In the next passage of play, in what was developing into a good spell for Brazil, Rivaldo and Ronaldo linked up again, with a superb backheel from Ronaldo providing acres of room for Leonardo after Calderwood slid desperately to block a shot from Ronaldo that did not arrive. Fortunately for Scotland, Leonardo's left-footed shot was woeful and jarred uncomfortably with the previous moment of Brazilian magic.

Next, the aerial presence of Durie unsettled Brazil and saw Gallacher free himself on the right wing after neat interplay with Lambert. Latching onto Lambert's pass, Gallacher provided yet another good cross into the Brazilian box, which Taffarel palmed out unconvincingly. The loose ball then struck Cafu, who knew little about it. So nearly an own goal – Brazil breathed an enormous sigh of relief as the ball trundled past the post with Taffarel helpless.

In the following exchanges, Scotland were on top, with the players looking absolutely confident and perhaps fancying themselves capable of an upset in this, the biggest match of their lives. Colin Hendry by now looked capable of heading balls all day long, with his right-hand man Calderwood strong in the tackle and composed on the ground. Boyd likewise provided speed and poise at the left centre-back position, providing additional cover for Dailly, who was increasingly breaking forwards to support the attack on the left. Craig Burley was putting in a similar shift on the right, and Lambert by now looked every inch the world-class defensive midfielder so treasured by Borussia Dortmund the season before last. Playing in a slightly more advanced central-midfield position, left-sided John Collins was Lambert's perfect midfield partner. Both were clever players who rarely wasted the ball, and their growing on-field understanding was apparent. It would not be an overstatement to say that Scotland were stronger in most areas of the pitch on the 60-minute mark, as constant chants of 'Scotland! Scotland!' could be heard from the knowledgeable Tartan Army, who could see that their team were well in the match.

Brazil, for all their stellar line-up, were by now reduced to less and less frequent spurts of magic as the half wore on and their superstars tired. Ronaldo was increasingly seen dropping deeper and deeper to try to influence the game, and to escape the towering defending of Hendry and Calderwood.

Then, on the 70-minute mark, a Brazil substitution changed the game. Zagallo introduced 20-year-old Denílson, the world's most expensive player, for Bebeto, who had been unable to exert any influence in the second half. As Denílson sprinted onto the pitch, the Brazilian team's energy levels changed immediately as they appeared to rediscover the extra gear that would ultimately provide them with just enough to break Scotland hearts. Suddenly, all Brazilian play was directed towards Denílson down the Brazilian left. This change of emphasis also provided an extra man for Carlos, who was a wonderful wing-back but had been matched on the day by an excellent performance by Burley.

Scotland initially received a warning, when Denílson collected the ball superbly on his chest and smashed a fierce left-footed shot at goal, which Leighton, who had not been troubled since Rivaldo's efforts early in the second half, saved well. As the teams reset, Leighton then cleared long, straight to Aldair, who immediately fed Denílson on Brazil's left touchline on the halfway line. Denílson then drew in Lambert and Calderwood, the latter having strayed a long way from his right centre-back position. Calderwood, usually superb in the tackle, committed to a sliding challenge, and in a moment of Brazilian genius, Denílson, fresh from the bench and sensing his moment, skipped away from both players and into acres of space. Denílson, now in full flow, backheeled to Rivaldo, who had also now sprung into life. Lambert, as you would expect, read the danger, and had the fitness to make up the ground. Lambert launched a slide tackle towards Rivaldo, who demanded a free kick from the referee. The referee instead played a good advantage, and Leonardo this time was quick to the loose ball, and again fed Denílson on the left wing. Scotland now looked ragged for the first time since early in the first half. This time, Burley had tracked Denílson, who shifted the ball onto his left foot, before checking back inside to roll the ball to Carlos, who had popped up at the corner of Scotland's penalty area to provide the overload. Carlos again exchanged passes with

Denílson, who in turn fed Rivaldo, who rolled the ball to Dunga, who had taken up the central attacking-midfield position. The Brazilian captain took one touch to control the ball before chipping a searching right-footed pass into Scotland's penalty area towards Cafu. With all the play having been concentrated on Brazil's left since Denílson's introduction, this quick switch to the right completely caught out Scotland's back line. Only Durie had sensed the danger early enough to get near Cafu, and he made an acrobatic effort to reach the ball, which agonisingly evaded his flying outstretched foot. Cafu was able to get a right-footed touch on the ball to send it goalwards. Leighton, in typical style, had also been quick to read the danger and raced off his line in a manner that had saved Scotland so many times before. Not this time. Leighton did indeed save Cafu's shot with his chest, but the ball ricocheted toward the helpless Boyd, who was six yards out and facing his own net. The ball cannoned off Boyd's upper right arm, with just enough power to bounce into Scotland's unguarded net ahead of Hendry, who fell to his knees in disbelief.

Cafu sprinted away, arms outstretched in celebration, and launched into an acrobatic forward somersault as his relieved team-mates mobbed him. Leighton, in a moment of gentlemanly class, showed his experience as he patted the dejected Boyd on the head. The goal had arrived in the 73rd minute, just three minutes after substitute Denílson's introduction.

In the final 17 minutes of play, Scotland rallied, but the defining moment of the match had come and gone. On 79 minutes, Craig Brown introduced Billy McKinlay for Jackson, and on 85 minutes Tosh McKinlay came on for Dailly. However, it would be unfair to evaluate the contribution of either substitute, such was the desperate nature of their late introduction. Commendably, Scotland were able to position themselves deep in Brazilian territory as the clock ran down, and two training-ground set pieces orchestrated by John Collins offered the Tartan Army late glimmers of hope that a draw might be achievable against the world champions. Most notably, a long-range right-footed volley from Craig Burley brought a save from Taffarel. In the end, however, it was just not meant to be for Scotland. José Maria García-Aranda blew the final whistle that broke Scottish hearts.

Full Time

Once again, the *World Cup Diary* captures the dressing-room scene at full time, with Alex Miller addressing the players about the frailties in the left-back area that have led to the second Brazilian goal. The dressing room is one of quiet reflection and frustration. Billy McKinlay, with his distinctive dyed-blond hair, sits in his match shorts with his arms folded. Kevin Gallacher looks absolutely disgusted as he peels off his socks and boots, and throws a sticking plaster on the dressing-room floor. Gordon Durie sits next to Gallacher, head down, with his hands covering his face, and a towel over his shoulders. Tom Boyd sits looking straight ahead with a vacant expression on his face. Darren Jackson, in a white Umbro vest and shorts, sits quietly reflecting. Typical of the coaches' communication style, Craig Brown then seamlessly follows Miller's evaluation, stating, 'You dug in well, lads. Very unfortunate. We've got to get the heads up. We've still got two games [we can win], which is very much within our capabilities.' The Scotland National Team now had six days to pick themselves up by their bootstraps and get ready for their next opponents.

10

NORWAY

Thursday 11 June 1998 was yet another warm, bright day in the South of France, and Scotland arrived at their St Rémy training pitch to a much livelier scene than usual. Man for man, Scotland had held their own against the famous *Seleção*, but ultimately preparations for the next match against Norway would now begin with no points on the board. As the players disembarked their usual France 98 coach, wearing their familiar white and black Umbro training gear, television cameras and journalists were scattered around the fringes of the car park of the small 1,500-capacity stadium. The impressive display in the Stade de France the day before had grabbed media attention, and today's training session was clearly deemed newsworthy.

Now the tournament was officially underway, local interest had also grown considerably, and the stadium was filled to capacity with families, schoolchildren and travelling fans from other nations. Although the Republic of Ireland had not qualified, a group of Irish fans in particular made their presence felt with choruses of 'Flower of

Scotland', while the French schoolchildren chanted, '*Allez l'Écosse!*' Those in attendance were treated to a full eleven-a-side match, with Gary McAllister refereeing, and Brown and Miller facing off against each other as opposing managers.

On return to the Valrugues Hotel, the players were then granted the afternoon and evening off for relaxation, and a large contingent of the squad opted to make the most of the continuous superb weather by sunbathing at the poolside and listening to music. Others preferred the shade, and the spacious and pleasant games room was also a popular choice. The players mingled and chatted with the backroom staff, and the atmosphere remained harmonious and professional.

After a similar day on Friday 12 June, it had been arranged for the squad to travel to Marseille to watch France's opening match of the tournament against South Africa. Emerging from their coach at the Stade Vélodrome, the Scottish delegation were, as usual, identical in their chosen uniform for the evening, which on this occasion comprised a blue Umbro sweatshirt, white polo shirt and black and white Umbro jacket emblazoned with the Scottish Gas logo. With their celebrity status growing, the players posed for pictures with security staff before entering the newly revamped home of Olympique de Marseille.

The home fans in the Stade Vélodrome were dressed for the occasion and in fine voice, albeit tinged with nervous anticipation. It should not be forgotten that, in 1998, France had not qualified for the World Cup since Mexico 86, and furthermore as hosts had not been required to qualify for this World Cup. This lack of recent World Cup credibility had bred scepticism about their chances of success among the French press and general public, and head coach Aimé Jacquet had struggled to alleviate the fears of the nation. On the evening of 12 June, France need not have worried, however, as they convincingly beat South Africa 3-0 with goals from Christophe Dugarry and Thierry Henry either side of an own goal.

Attending such an important match in a carnival atmosphere was yet another memorable experience for the Scotland players, and a perfect example of the high value placed by Craig Brown on this type of 'squad night out'. There can be little doubt that Brown was a football fan at heart who built squad morale not only on the training pitch but by rewarding dedication and professionalism with enjoyable experiences. Paul Lambert corroborates this view in *A Bhoy's Own Story*, writing that he enjoyed the break and being part of the 55,000-capacity Marseille crowd. Lambert recalls that the Scotland players ran a 'first scorer' sweepstake, before dispatching Billy McKinlay and Darren Jackson for some food, the pair returning not only with the snacks but also their faces painted in the red, white and blue of France!

It was back to business on Saturday 13 June, and some players went to see physiotherapist Eric Ferguson in the specially-adapted treatment room in the Valrugues Hotel prior to the day's training session. They arrived at the St Rémy facilities later in the morning to more noisy scenes, thanks to France's resounding success in Marseille the previous evening. This victory had generated a mixture of relief and elation among the French, and prompted increased enthusiasm and ownership of the tournament among the local population. The small stadium was now swamped with autograph hunters and fans requesting photographs, and Scotland's players were more than happy to oblige, spending several minutes at the end of the training session speaking to the locals and ensuring they left the stadium happy.

The afternoon followed the similar pattern of poolside sunbathing, pool competitions, video games and watching the World Cup itself. Then, in the evening, in the familiar surroundings of the comfortable, darkened meeting room, Craig Brown and Alex Miller led an in-depth tactical meeting, at the conclusion of which the players would learn the team to face the Norwegians three days later. Paul Lambert recalls at this stage that the team had already studied footage of Norway's 2–2 draw with Morocco in their opening group match, and also Norway's shock 4–2 friendly victory over Brazil in Oslo in May 1997. Alex Miller reminded the players of Norway's central threat on goal before Brown, standing adjacent to his flipchart at the front of the room, got ready to deliver the team news. One of Brown's concerns was also whether the attacking threat would come from 'the big player', meaning towering striker Tore André Flo, or if Ole Gunnar Solskjær might play, in which case, 'the diagonal ball is not going to be a threat then'. However, Brown's 'major concern' was that Scotland approached the match in the 'right frame of mind'. Therefore, Brown told the players, Scotland would start with exactly the same team as they had against Brazil.

On Sunday 14 June, the media-savvy Brown invited the Scottish football journalists to a buffet lunch with the players at the Valrugues Hotel. Yet again, there was not a cloud in the sky as sunburnt journalists in shades and light shirts mingled with the players and backroom staff in the pleasant surroundings. The afternoon also included a presentation for John Collins for achieving 50 caps and Darren Jackson for achieving 25 caps. Their team-mates applauded and cheered them both as SFA President Jack

McGinn presented them with their well deserved engraved medals.

In *Adventures in the Golden Age*, Archie Macpherson, who was in France as a correspondent and TV commentator for Eurosport, sums up that Scotland had acquitted themselves splendidly against the world champions in Paris, which had created an enhanced sense of wellbeing during this period of the trip. Macpherson also suggests that Scotland were confident in their preparations for the Norway match because they knew a great deal about their opponents, which in no small part was due to the nucleus of Norway's squad being made up of English-based players, as Scotland's was to some extent, details of which I discuss further on in this chapter.

Nonetheless, the Norway of this era were a tricky proposition. Led by Egil Olsen, who had taken over as head coach in 1990, Norway had now qualified for only their third World Cup finals, but their second in a row. During this period of unprecedented success under the pragmatic Olsen, Norway had climbed as high as second in the FIFA world rankings, so there was little doubt Scotland were in for a difficult afternoon in Bordeaux.

Parallels can be drawn when you consider the direction Norwegian and Scottish football had taken during this period, and likewise when you compare the careers of Egil Olsen and Craig Brown. Like Brown, Olsen was a Physical Education graduate, who had first taught in a university before progressing to a position with the Norwegian Football Association. In an almost identical trajectory towards international management, Olsen had also managed

Norway's Under-21 team before landing the role of first-team head coach.

However, Brown and Olsen's paths separated when it came to football methods and tactics. As discussed in the first chapter of this book, Brown had taught tactical flexibility when working for the SFA at Inverclyde. Indeed, this principle was a cornerstone of Brown's philosophy. In *The Game of My Life*, Brown states, 'I have my own thoughts and systems, but I am always prepared to have any aspect of my knowledge of the game improved by sensible suggestions,' and goes on to claim that he has never seen a successful long-term coach who wasn't 'prepared to adapt, adopt and try to improve'.

Olsen, on the other hand, was a leading exponent of a direct brand of football from which he did not deviate. Olsen will forever be identified with the long-ball game, and in *Inverting the Pyramid: The History of Football Tactics*, Jonathan Wilson considers Olsen's tactical influences as having been inspired by the work of Englishman Charles Reep, who published a paper in 1968 with statistician Bernard Benjamin in the *Journal of the Royal Statistical Society* entitled *Skill and Chance in Association Football*. Reep's study boasted analysis of patterns of play covering a 14-year period between 1953 and 1967, the conclusions of which had captivated Olsen. Pre-dating smartphones and computers, Reep had applied his mathematical formulae by attending live football and recording his results in shorthand. Wilson cites that Reep had concluded that 91.5 per cent of goals were scored from moves of three passes or fewer, and that a goal was scored approximately once in every nine shots.

Of course, Reep's tactical analysis is rudimentary when considered against the backdrop of contemporary football data analysis. Increasingly, any football fan interested in this field can obtain vast amounts of statistics from a range of websites, and it is usual that top professional clubs will have teams of analysts drawing reports from statistics provided by global data companies like Opta Sports. Nonetheless, Reep, despite his conclusions arguably advocating an 'ugly' version of football, was undoubtedly decades ahead of his time, a fact not lost on the academic Egil Olsen. Indeed, in *Inverting the Pyramid*, Wilson states that Olsen and Reep wrote to each other in the 1990s when Olsen was revolutionising Norwegian football. On the eve of the tournament, when asked by *World Soccer* to explain his tactical plans for France 98, Olsen stuck to his opinion that the 'penetrative direct style' was 'the most effective' and that they would adhere to it, 'even though many countries, including England, are going in the opposite direction'.

These fascinating remarks possibly refer to Graham Taylor's resignation as England manager in 1993, the same year that Olsen's success with Norway began to gather momentum. Like Olsen, Taylor was also heavily influenced by the Reepian model when managing Watford in the 1980s, and *Inverting the Pyramid* cites an interview with Reep in Scottish football magazine *The Punter*, in which Reep stated that Taylor had phoned him several times to discuss styles of play during his tenure with Watford. *World Soccer* pressed Olsen further on his tactical thoughts ahead of France 98, highlighting criticism of Norway's direct style of play. Olsen's retort was, 'If you play a ball beyond two, three, four opponents and then create a sort of unbalance [sic], people tend to play the ball backwards again… you give them a chance to restore the balance. It's an easy philosophy: when you have created an unbalance [sic], don't let them restore it.'

Interestingly, in *A Bhoy's Own Story*, Paul Lambert recalls his main distraction at France 98 also related directly to Egil Olsen. Lambert had been impressed with Celtic's 1997–98 title-winning manager Wim Jansen, and concedes during his World Cup preparations to being extremely disappointed to learn of Jansen's shock departure from Celtic. Lambert recalls that he and his Celtic team-mates pondered over the long list of supposed candidates being touted in the newspapers at the time, ranging from Leicester City manager Martin O'Neill to Carlos Alberta Parreira, at France 98 with his Saudi Arabia team, and well-travelled Dutch coach Aad de Mos. Lambert states that one name in particular kept cropping up that 'sent a shudder of apprehension' down his spine: Egil Olsen. While trying to train and prepare in St Rémy, Lambert convinced himself that there was no smoke without fire, and Olsen must be a frontrunner for the Celtic job. 'The news went down like the *Titanic* as far as the Celtic lads in France were concerned,' Lambert states in *A Bhoy's Own Story*. 'We like to think we know how Celtic play the game. Traditionally, the club has always played attractive, attacking football... Mr Olsen, on the other hand, prefers to play a long-ball game, and when you watch Norway perform to his style, you can't possibly say that they are an attractive team to look at.' Lambert goes on to say that he and Craig Burley had discussed this at length in France and 'weren't exactly relishing the prospect of Olsen taking over'. Incidentally, their fears were unfounded, and Slovakian coach Dr Jozef Venglos was confirmed as Celtic's new managerial appointment in July 1998.

As mentioned, Norway's primary threat arose from tall Chelsea striker Tore André Flo, who to date is Rangers' most expensive signing, later arriving in Scotland from Chelsea for £12 million in November 2000. And, of course, Norway boasted Manchester United striker Ole Gunnar Solskjær, who had scored 18 goals in 25 league games for Manchester United in 1996–97, but who had been less effective in 1997–98 due to injuries. Like Scotland, Norway had a resolute defence, marshalled by Ronny Johnsen and Henning Berg, also both of Manchester United, and Stig Inge Bjørnebye of Liverpool. Berg had also been a defensive partner of Colin Hendry's at Blackburn Rovers during their English Premier League title-winning campaign of 1994–95, and goalkeeper Frode Grodås was a clubmate of Colin Calderwood's at Tottenham, so, as previously touched on, there was a level of familiarity between the two squads. Despite criticism of their direct style of play, Norway had out-trumped Scotland's superb defensive record during France 98 qualification, emerging unbeaten from their group after conceding only two goals.

Later on that Sunday of 14 June, after the Scottish press had departed the Valrugues Hotel, Craig Brown led another in-depth tactical analysis of Norway, which would guide the final training session at St Rémy before departure for Bordeaux. As we know by now, Brown was no green recruit in the tactical battlefield, and he had evidently studied Norway intensively in preparation for this crucial team talk. As usual, the players listened intently from their comfortable chairs in the darkened room, with Brown and Alex Miller prowling either side of their tactical flipchart.

Specifically, Brown had identified a potential threat from long diagonal balls played by left-back Bjørnebye towards the head of striker Flo, who was taller than any Scottish defender at 6ft 4in (1.93m). Brown instructed attack-minded wing-back Craig Burley to assume an orthodox right-back position when Norway deployed this tactic. Brown acknowledged that this was in some ways contrary to the team's instinctive counter-attacking style, which sought to release the wing-backs at every opportunity. Brown therefore created an eleven-man team comprising the reserve squad members to replicate Norway in the training session. Brown positioned his tallest outfield reserve player, centre-back Matt Elliott, as the reserve team's striker, to replicate Norway's Flo. Brown acknowledged the 'brilliant' attitude of the reserves in the squad whose real-world playing chances would be limited but whose role in this training set-up would be vital. Tosh McKinlay, playing for the reserves, would deliver diagonal balls to the Scotland first team's left-back position so that Christian Dailly would perceive the threat and get back goalside. Brown indicated where Tom Boyd, Colin Calderwood and Craig Burley would be positioned across the back line, before adding, 'If everyone's switched on here, as we should be, it's half an hour's job.'

On Monday 15 June, there was an early rise for the players, with another short coach trip to Nîmes Airport and a flight to Bordeaux. Security adviser George Dickson oversaw the loading of the squad's extensive luggage and equipment into hired vans outside the hotel to be transported to Bordeaux by road, while the players began to emerge in their shades and shorts with their lighter hand luggage. As usual, Brown's trusted backroom team had delivered on their required targets, and the operation was running like clockwork. The coach journey passed without incident, and once onboard the Air France Boeing 747 (with France 98 livery, of course) Craig Brown calmly addressed his *World Cup Diary*, commenting that the 'guys' were 'in a relaxed frame of mind' and that the squad were looking forward to lunch in their Bordeaux hotel and watching the England match against Tunisia on television once they arrived.

Meanwhile, the Tartan Army were also streaming into Bordeaux in their thousands. Scotland fan Martin Riddell, a veteran of dozens of Scotland awaydays around the world, talked to the *Official Scotland Podcast* about the 'incredible' atmosphere. 'All Scandinavian fans have been fantastic any time I've been to any of those countries,' Riddell told the podcast, 'and the Norwegians are no different.' Very much like Scottish fans, Riddell added, 'there's a lot of families go, a lot of groups of friends. No trouble at all.'

As the players arrived at their city-centre hotel headquarters, they were greeted by the superb rhythmical sounds of the MacUmba band, who had set up in the street to welcome the delegation. The Bordeaux locals had stopped and gathered in droves to listen to the blend of Scottish bagpipes and Brazilian Samba percussion, creating a spectacular street scene as the players disembarked from the coach. While it is certain that the squad appreciated this incredible welcome, they swiftly entered the hotel in a focused procession, with seemingly little else on their minds other than refuelling their bodies in advance of their training session in the afternoon. Later, once inside on the Parc de Lescure pitch, the players required little motivation for their session in the superb surroundings. Like every host stadium, the Parc de Lescure was in supreme condition following its multi-million-pound refit, and it was a beautiful afternoon in Bordeaux. Goalkeepers Jim Leighton, Neil Sullivan and Jonathan Gould stood out from the outfielders in their bright red training tops, and the players were separated into small sides using orange and yellow bibs. Craig Brown looked completely relaxed as his operation ticked over smoothly in front of him. With Alex Miller on the prowl on his behalf, he was confident there would be no let-up in training standards, and from the pitch he again found time to address his *World Cup Diary*, commenting positively on the fine, ambient weather conditions, impressive facilities and excellent playing surface.

In the meantime, the Tartan Army's invasion of Bordeaux was gaining momentum, and the party was now in full swing. In *Adventures in the Golden Age*, Archie Macpherson recollects travelling to Bordeaux from Marseille, where he had been commentating for Eurosport on England's 2–0 victory over Tunisia on Monday 15 June. Macpherson had witnessed a poisonous atmosphere in Marseille, with crowd trouble marring the fixture, and recalls the contrast of the carnival atmosphere in Bordeaux on his arrival the next day. Macpherson recalls walking through the city, where the Scotland fans were behaving like a peace corps compared to what he had witnessed in Marseille, with the Norwegians and Scots mixing like nations with a common heritage.

The *Scotsport Extra Time* YouTube channel shows incredible camcorder footage captured in Bordeaux on Tuesday 16 June. One member of the Tartan Army swigs Bordeaux red wine straight from the bottle, accompanied by several acquaintances also enjoying the fine wine, which they inform the camera cost £23.50 for the bottle, from plastic cups. The interviewees compare the world-renowned Bordeaux red to Buckfast tonic wine, some stating that they prefer the latter. As in Paris just a week before, the scene is colourful, with brand-new Scotland replica shirts worn with kilts, and shoulders draped in flags bearing the blue and white of the St Andrew's cross. The bright yellow Scotland away shirt, a popular choice of garment for spectators at the previous match against Brazil, is also in evidence. A tented village serving Tennent's Lager has been erected for the occasion in the city centre, and the footage captures bare-chested Scots drinking as they dance to the World Cup anthem, 'Carnaval de Paris' by Dario G, which, with its famous bagpipe solo in the middle, is by now inescapable at every venue. Little wonder that, according to Martin Riddell, the Mayor of Bordeaux placed an advert in the Scottish newspapers thanking the Scottish fans for being there and turning it 'into just one massive party'.

Tickets are, of course, the currency, with those who have them happy to flash them to the camera. Other, ticketless fans discuss how much they would be willing to pay. Five hundred pounds trips off the tongue of one hopeful, suggesting that black-market prices have come down by two-thirds since Paris, where Archie Macpherson witnessed last-minute tickets changing hands for £1,500 each.

Meanwhile, within Scotland's Bordeaux hotel headquarters, as instructed the previous day, the players made their way to their 11.30 meeting on the morning of the match. The day's casual uniform consisted of a bright lime-green Umbro training top, by far the loudest colour choice so far, and fitting with the bright colourful party in full swing outside on the city streets. It was down to business once again for Craig Brown in the hotel function suite as he addressed his players as a group for the final time prior to departing for Parc de Lescure. Brown was again captured on his *World Cup Diary*, stating that the squad must 'prepare professionally' for this 'vital game', and that he wanted 'everybody up for it, and wanting to put a shift in'. Win this game, Brown was suggesting, and Scotland would be right in the qualifying mix.

A short time later, the players appeared dressed in their navy suits ahead of the coach departure to shuttle them to the nearby Parc de Lescure. As they filtered out to the street, the hired vans created a deliberate barrier between the hotel and coach entrance, which allowed the players to board without being spotted by those enjoying the festivities. Due to the heat, the players removed their suit jackets on the coach, revealing royal blue shirts and navy ties. Prior to departing, the *World Cup Diary* shows the players engaging with a stray member of the Tartan Army wearing a 'C U Jimmy' hat (inspired by Russ Abbot's comic stereotype of a Scotsman, 'C U Jimmy', on his BBC TV shows in the 1980s) and beard through the coach window. The players laughed loudly as the stray fan gave the players a defiant wave and thumbs-up, before purposefully taking off again in the direction of the party.

On arrival at the stadium, on a large table in the changing room, the backroom staff busily laid out Scotland's yellow away shirts, which Brown later explained Scotland were instructed to wear due to a substantial proportion of the world's audience still watching the World Cup on black and white televisions, even in 1998. Scotland's bright yellow away shirts added yet another colour dimension to the increasingly bright spectacle in Bordeaux, and all that remained now were the warm-up and team talk.

With the party now having moved to the stadium, the 35,000-capacity Parc de Lescure was packed to the rafters as the two teams filed out onto the pitch to a cacophony of noise. Scotland, in their yellow shirts, navy shorts and red socks faced the Norwegians in their red shirts, white shorts and black socks. On commentary duty for Eurosport, Archie Macpherson described the scene as a sea of colour, with fans mixing together, creating an incredible atmosphere, and capturing the true spirit of World Cup football.

Norway had made three changes from their 2-2 draw with Morocco, with Erik Mykland, Øyvind Leonhardsen and Ole Gunnar Solksjær replaced by Roar Strand, Ståle Solbakken and Vidar Riseth. Later reflecting on his omission from this starting line-up with *FourFourTwo*, Solskjær said, 'The [1998] World Cup was strange for me. I was taken off after 45 minutes against Morocco, I didn't play the second game and then I came on against Brazil.'

As mentioned, Scotland's starting 3-5-2 formation was unchanged from that of their opening match six days previously.

In order of squad numbers, the Scotland team named to face Norway on 16 June 1998 were as follows: Jim Leighton (1); Tom Boyd (3); Colin Calderwood (4); Colin Hendry (5); Kevin Gallacher (7); Craig Burley (8); Gordon Durie (9); Darren Jackson (10); John Collins (11); Paul Lambert (14); Christian Dailly (22).

In order of squad numbers, the Norway team in their 4-5-1 formation were as follows: Frode Grodås (1); Ronny Johnsen (3); Henning Berg (4); Stig Inge Bjørnebye (5); Ståle Solbakken (6); Tore André Flo (9); Kjetil Rekdal (10); Dan Eggen (15); Havard Flo (17); Vidar Riseth (21); Roar Strand (22).

First Half

At 5.30pm local time, after the coin toss and national anthems, Scotland versus Norway had arrived. Scotland kicked off in their usual manner, launching an early diagonal ball towards a wing-back breaking forwards. Christian Dailly rose to meet the ball with his head, but it cannoned too far for Scotland to retrieve and ran through to Norwegian captain and goalkeeper Frode Grodås. Grodås immediately launched a long kick, which Norway won in the air inside Scotland's half. A throw-in quickly followed for Norway, still inside Scotland's half, which was taken by left-back Stig Inge Bjørnebye, and again Norway won possession in the air before Colin Hendry cleared. Within the first minute, Norway had firmly demonstrated their aerial prowess, and it was already abundantly clear that they were a vastly different proposition from Brazil.

It was Scotland who next made their presence felt with some bustling play from Gordon Durie, who was clearly far from intimidated by the physicality of the Norwegians. Durie was then furious with referee László Vágner when Vágner did not award a corner following a tussle with Ronny Johnsen. The Hungarian referee reprimanded Durie for dissent, and the player soon calmed down when faced with the prospect of an early yellow card.

From the resulting goal kick, Grodås again went long, and this time Vidar Riseth won the header inside Scotland's half. In terms of Norway's shape, Riseth had started on the left of their five-man midfield, and also seemed to be the player tasked with advancing where possible in support of striker Tore André Flo. Ole Gunnar Solskjær appeared to have been sacrificed for this purpose. Once again, Norway won a throw-in on their left flank, and Bjørnebye advanced deep into Scotland territory to take the throw and support the attack.

Norway were on top in the very early exchanges, with particular progress made on Scotland's right, where Kevin Gallacher then ruffled Norwegian feathers with a firm challenge on Riseth. Much to Riseth's discontent, the exchange resulted in a Scotland free kick, causing Riseth momentarily to retaliate, and he became the next player to receive a reprimand from referee Vágner.

Craig Burley and John Collins then wasted no time taking a quick free kick and making up good ground on Scotland's right. Collins turned onto his favoured left foot, shaping up to cross, but then checked back unexpectedly onto his right, outfoxing his tracker Ståle Solbakken. Collins then crossed superbly with his weaker right foot after spotting a late run from left wing-back Dailly, who was the only player to read the situation. Dailly connected with the cross perfectly with his head, heading downwards into the turf, with Grodås stranded in the Norwegian goal. Unfortunately for Scotland, the ball whizzed past the Norwegians' left post, with Dailly outdone by the narrowness of the angle. This was a good early chance for Scotland, which had resulted from some decent football. The Norwegian defence, usually so solid, felt the wrath of captain Grodås, who had been left exposed.

In the subsequent passages of play, it came as no surprise that long-ball exponents Norway continued to punt long searching balls from defence towards the head of Tore André Flo and Riseth. Hendry in particular was relishing the aerial battle, and with Scotland's defence generally very strong in the air, it appeared Norway's fairly one-dimensional attacking tactics might not overly trouble Scotland. Even so, Norway were also extremely combative in midfield, and continually broke up the play of Collins, Paul Lambert and Darren Jackson as they tried to build from the back after gathering the second ball.

Durie and Kevin Gallacher were also putting in their usual running shift, continually dropping into advanced midfield positions to link the play, thus giving Norway's centre-back pairing of Johnsen and Dan Eggen plenty to think about. Henning Berg, a competent centre-back, was deployed at right back by Norway, where he appeared slightly less comfortable. In the first ten minutes of the match, it was also evident that Dailly was in the mood, with his continual roving runs from the left wing-back position giving Berg a problem. The Tartan Army were encouraged by what they were seeing so far, and echoes of, 'Scotland! Scotland!' rang around the Parc de Lescure.

As the half wore on, Hendry easily won more headers, allowing Lambert to collect the ball from Colin Calderwood and Tom Boyd in the central defensive-midfield position to build from the back. Similarly to the Brazil match, Lambert's economical play naturally brought Collins and Jackson into the match in their slightly more advanced midfield positions. This in turn provided opportunity for link up play with either wing-back, or with Gallacher and Durie dropping deeper.

The next major chance of the first half also fell to Scotland. Lambert initially dropped deep to link with Boyd, providing Boyd with the time and space to fire a long, accurate, searching pass towards Gallacher, who had run the left channel. Gallacher, tracked by Berg, was able to reach the ball first, and spoon an awkward first-time, left-footed cross into the Norwegian penalty area from wide on the left. Despite the attentions of Johnsen and Bjørnebye, Durie rose highest in the box, hanging in the air as the ball met his forehead. Again, Grodås was left stranded in the Norway goal, as Durie's floated header appeared to loop towards the top-left corner, drifting marginally over the top. The Tartan Army, sniffing a goal, then cheered in encouragement, rallying their team to try again.

With Jim Leighton in Scotland's goal virtually a spectator, Egil Olsen's game of mathematical averages suddenly clicked for Norway. The athletic Riseth won the ball in the left-wing position after another long kick from Grodås, taking Burley out of the equation on Scotland's right. Tore André Flo, who for a big man was surprisingly good with the ball at his feet, collected the ball and held the play up nicely. With things developing into the exact scenario that Craig Brown had feared beforehand, Flo then knocked the ball back to Bjørnebye, in the left-back position, who fired a long diagonal ball towards Harvard Flo on Norway's right wing. Harvard Flo then outjumped Dailly, directing a header into Scotland's penalty area. Without the ball bouncing, the onrushing Roar Strand won yet another header for Norway, and suddenly Scotland were exposed, with the ball now loose inside the penalty box. No other Norwegian was following in on the ball to take this gilt-edged chance to open the scoring and, fortunately for Scotland, the ball ran through the box harmlessly for Burley to collect. It was a warning nonetheless, and the precise scenario Brown had identified as a threat and drilled his team to suppress. The outcome might also have been different had the predatory Solksjær been on the pitch.

Positively for Scotland, this example of the danger posed by Norway did not alter the complexion of the game, with Scotland increasingly dominant as the first half wore on. The eccentric Olsen, sporting his usual trademark wellington boots for the occasion, looked pensive on the

Norway bench. Norwegian captain Grodås, wearing a bright blue captain's armband over his striking red, yellow and black goalkeeper top, barked motivational instructions at his team in front of him.

Then came the biggest moment of the first half. The irrepressible Durie took a long throw-in into the Norwegian penalty box from Scotland's right, which Hendry won but could not direct goalwards. Durie, remaining in the right-wing position, then collected the second ball for Scotland and moved into the Norway penalty box with the ball at his feet. Bjørnebye, positioned poorly, was caught on the wrong side of Durie, and clattered clumsily into the Scotland forward, sending him sprawling onto the turf. The referee blew his whistle for what seemed like a certain penalty, but to Durie's dismay the animated Hungarian referee sprinted over to the area of the incident to award the foul outside the box. On replays, it looked a poor decision, and in the modern era of video-assisted refereeing, a penalty would most likely have been awarded to Scotland. From the resulting free kick, Collins and Lambert attempted a rehearsed routine, but the Norwegians cleared and the chance had gone.

By now the Tartan Army were in fine voice, singing loudly in the afternoon sun. With Hendry completely dominating the aerial duels, and with every Scotland player playing to their maximum potential, it was beginning to seem like a win for Craig Brown's men might be on the cards in Bordeaux.

However, like Scotland, the Norway of this era proved resilient opposition, and the next chance of the match fell to the Scandinavians. Grodås started the passage of play with a long kick out, which Boyd collected but did no more than to boot back downfield. Norway then drove at Scotland on the deck, catching Brown's men 'unbalanced', to use the words of Egil Olsen. With Scotland's defence wrong-footed, energetic midfielder Solbakken played an accurate pass toward his midfield partner Strand, who had stolen into Scotland's penalty box behind the defensive line. Strand then collected the pass brilliantly on his chest and fired a left-footed shot at Scotland's goal, with Hendry lunging unsuccessfully in an attempt to block the shot. Fortunately for Scotland, Leighton, as usual, had raced off his line to narrow the angle, and made a great stop with his midriff. Dailly then collected the loose ball and carried it to safety, with Scotland left to breathe a sigh of relief.

This passage of play encapsulated the first half, as, although Scotland appeared to have the upper hand, Norway's relentless application of Olsen's tactical plan undoubtedly created chances, with easily enough quality in their team to make one of them count sooner or later. The last significant passages of play in the first half led to a Solbakken volley that flew over the top after he combined well once again with Strand, and another Dailly header that Strand cleared off the line after a well-worked corner routine involving Collins and Gallacher.

Half Time

It took almost two minutes to walk from the pitch to the dressing rooms within the Parc de Lescure, and bizarrely the *World Cup Diary* captures the players and backroom staff running along the stadium corridors to maximise the half-time break. Once settled and seated, Craig Brown and Alex Miller stood behind a large table on which sat bottles of water and cups. The players sat in silence, taking fluids on board, with some such as Colin Calderwood and Tom Boyd stripped to the waist with their boots removed. Gordon Durie stood drinking with a steely look of determination etched on his face. Brown then addressed his players, complimenting their 'tremendous first 20 minutes' of 'brilliant play', which 'was exactly what we asked you to do'. Brown added that Scotland just had to keep good possession, get the ball earlier to the front men, and make better use of Burley on the right.

Seamlessly as usual, Miller then began to speak just as Brown finished, adding, 'This is your international. Honestly. I tell ye, you're going to win. Hey. Believe in yourselves. We're going to win it.' Miller's motivational words provoked a rousing response among the players, who began to shout, 'C'mon lads!' Brown joined in, shouting, 'C'mon. No hard luck stories here... We've got to get this goal.'

Second Half

Norway kicked off for the second half, and immediately shoved the ball out to right-back Henning Berg, who lofted the ball forwards. Scotland initially cleared the ball, but neat play in the Norway midfield freed Vidar Riseth wide on the left, who was then able to shift the ball deftly outside onto his left foot, evading Colin Calderwood, shifting across to cover. This created the half-yard Riseth needed to send in an absolute beauty of a left-footed cross. Norway's electric start to the second half had caught Christian Dailly completely cold, and time seemed to stand still for Scotland as Harvard Flo then arrived at Jim Leighton's back post to stoop and head Riseth's superb cross into the gaping net. There were only 29 seconds on the second-half clock.

With Leighton despondent, the jubilant Norwegians mobbed Flo, and goalkeeper Frode Grodås held his arms aloft, cheerleading the Norwegian fans, who had erupted around the stadium. Scotland had paid the ultimate price for a significant lapse in concentration, and now they had a mountain to climb.

Following the restart, the Norwegian goal had noticeably rocked Scotland's confidence and self-belief, and conversely had a galvanising effect on the Norwegians, who had been under par until their breakthrough. Tore André Flo was now looking like the player Scotland had feared as he gathered in the ball at his feet and twisted and turned. Norwegian number ten Kjetil Rekdal, who had had a quiet first period, was now looking composed in midfield as Norway smelled blood.

The committed running of Dailly, who was having a fine game until his lapse that had led to the goal, offered respite for Scotland on the left, characterised by marauding runs into Norwegian territory. Even so, Norway's passing in the second half's early exchanges was crisp and accurate, and a second Norway half-chance arrived just a few minutes later, when Tore André Flo's long legs caught out Calderwood, robbing him of the ball, leading to Norway almost getting in behind Scotland's defence once more. Paul Lambert had tracked back and he snuffed out the danger on this occasion.

In the next significant passage of play, Scotland's unfortunate start to the second half got worse. With Norway looking more composed coming out of defence, Berg lofted another accurate pass toward Roar Strand, who collected the ball in acres of room on Norway's right wing. With Dailly caught forward on Scotland's left, Strand had the time and space to pick out a cross with his right foot, which initially looked dangerous but marginally evaded everyone in the penalty area. However, as the ball had flown across the danger area, Tore André Flo had clattered through the back of Calderwood, who had stood his ground inside the six-yard box. In a moment of cruel bad lack for Calderwood, he collided awkwardly with Riseth as he fell, and he was now clearly in distress.

Calderwood was initially treated on the pitch and decided to play on, but was noticeably clutching his bandaged right arm when play restarted. As dreadful as this was for Calderwood, it seemed that the injury to one of their on-field lieutenants had woken Scotland up in the passages of play that followed. Suddenly, Scotland were linking up again, and a superb pass from Lambert led to an equally impressive volleyed pass from Kevin Gallacher to Gordon Durie, who laid back to Craig Burley. Burley then spread the play wide, aiming for Dailly, who won a throw-in deep inside the Norway half. Dailly quickly took the throw to John Collins, who laid it back again to Dailly. Dailly then hit a good cross that drew Grodås a long way off his line, into an area where he did not want to be. Grodås, so assured in the first half, unexpectedly spilled the ball from his hands at the feet of Darren Jackson, before recovering and punching the ball to safety. This was encouraging for Scotland, but Calderwood, wincing in pain, had now signalled to the referee and the Scotland bench. In hindsight, this was unsurprising: Calderwood had broken his right hand, and his World Cup was over.

On 59 minutes, David Weir was introduced as a straight swap for Calderwood at the right centre-back position. Significantly, just prior to the substitution, Jackson had received a yellow card for a late tackle on Ronny Johnsen. This was Jackson's second booking in two matches, and he was now suspended for the third match against Morocco. For the first time in the tournament, Craig Brown decided to shuffle his pack, and two minutes later he also withdrew Jackson for Jackie McNamara, and moved Burley into Jackson's midfield position.

With Burley in midfield, and his Celtic clubmate McNamara at right wing-back, Scotland instantly looked more dangerous. In the same phase, Egil Olsen also withdrew goalscorer Harvard Flo and introduced Jahn Ivar Jakobsen, but Olsen's substitution did little to redress the balance. McNamara had clearly been straining at the leash from the bench, and began running at Norway at every opportunity down Scotland's right. With Burley also now breaking the shackles, and in his preferred position, Scotland looked a different team.

On 64 minutes, Norway gained a temporary reprieve via a corner won by Tore André Flo from Lambert after a long punt forward by Grodås. Scotland defended the corner effectively, but Flo recovered Durie's chipped clearance, and twisted and turned in his familiar style. But he had not bargained for Burley, who tackled him strongly and robbed him of the ball. Immediately Lambert brought the fresh legs of McNamara into the game once more, and the Celtic wing-back sprinted forward with the ball at his feet, with support from Weir, who also appeared to have licence to get forwards. Receiving the ball back from McNamara, Weir was fouled, but Collins was alive as usual, taking a quick free kick to keep up the momentum.

Temporarily, Scotland's positive play on the right broke down, as Norway won a throw-in that they launched in the direction of Flo, who made for the Scotland byline. Looking sure to retain possession, Flo was then halted by superb play from Lambert, who not only robbed Flo but skilfully kept the ball alive to allow Scotland to build from the back once more. Lambert then fed Dailly, who took off down

Scotland's left, tracked by Strand, who momentarily halted Scotland's left wing-back with a tackle that sent the ball back towards Scotland's defenders. Scotland retained possession with Hendry, who shoved the ball out to his new right centre-back partner Weir, who advanced towards the halfway line with his head up, looking for a passing option.

In a moment of superb execution, which provided Craig Brown with the perfect example of his favourite pass in football, Weir then split Norway's centre-backs Johnsen and Dan Eggen with a precision pass. Burley, whose shift into midfield just five minutes beforehand had altered the match so dramatically, had read Weir's pass a spilt second before anyone else, and had darted between the two centre-backs. In undoubtedly one of Scotland's all-time most memorable World Cup moments, Burley reached the ball first and hit a superb first-time, right-footed lob over the helpless Grodås into the Norwegian net. Burley spun away in ecstasy as the Tartan Army in Bordeaux finally had their moment to celebrate. Burley whacked the corner flag in a release of pure adrenaline and was caught first by McNamara, who jumped on his back. As he was mobbed by the rest of his team-mates Burley flashed a toothless grin to the camera. When later reflecting on these famous moments for *FourFourTwo*, the charismatic Burley stated, 'It was awesome when it went in, although I didn't look awesome the next day. There was a photo of me celebrating with no front teeth. The headline was, "Fangs a Million!" But it kept us in the tournament.'

In *A Bhoy's Own Story*, Paul Lambert also gives his evaluation of these passages of play. 'We needed a break, and we got one – even if it wasn't the kind we wanted!' Lambert said of Calderwood's broken hand and consequent substitution. 'The net result of all that was a terrific equaliser from Craig

[Burley], who latched onto a great ball from David [Weir] and scored a superb goal.'

For the final 24 minutes of the match, Scotland were absolutely rampant, and thoroughly deserved to score a winner. Norway weathered wave after wave of Scotland pressure, with Burley absolutely everywhere after his positional shift into central midfield. Indeed, Burley's powerful play breaking between the lines almost resulted in him grabbing a famous winner only minutes after his first goal. The chance was the culmination of the best move of the entire match, which involved the tireless Gallacher laying the ball back to Burley, who then played a superb one-two with Durie. Burley, for whom everything was coming off at this stage, spun away from his marker, and received Durie's return pass in space just outside the Norway penalty area. This time, Burley smashed a right-footed shot towards the top corner, before a tremendous one-handed save by Grodås rescued a point for Norway. Had this shot hit the net, Burley's performance in Bordeaux might have been remembered as the greatest ever for Scotland in a World Cup match.

Full Time

In the dressing room after the match, Craig Brown was captured on his *World Cup Diary* addressing the players positively about their 'magnificent performance' saying that they could still make it to the knockout stages with the vital 'wee victory' now required against Morocco in the final group game.

However, Paul Lambert sums up the general mood in the Scotland camp after the match in *A Bhoy's Own Story*, lamenting that, 'When the time came, we murdered them –

and yet it ended in a 1–1 draw. It was criminal.' Lambert, as mentioned previously when it looked like Egil Olsen might be bringing his brand of football to Celtic, clearly hated Norway's style. 'We played all the football and Norway didn't,' Lambert moans. Their football was 'horrible to play against and, I would imagine, pretty awful to watch'. Lambert adds that 'the Norwegians celebrated because they knew they had got out of jail'. Scotland had outplayed them all over the park and yet it had only been a draw. 'Naturally,' Lambert concludes, 'we were a bit upset.'

11

MOROCCO

After a long night of travel back to St Rémy, Craig Brown's disappointed squad were given a welcome day off on Wednesday 17 June, which some players used for a game of golf. Positively, Brazil's convincing 3–0 victory over Morocco in Saint-Etienne in the late match on 16 June had ensured Scotland still had something to play for, thus avoiding an undeserved elimination after just two matches. With two victories out of two, Brazil had now won the group outright with a game to spare, with Norway second on two points, and Morocco and Scotland tied on one point each. The downside was that second-round qualification was no longer in Scotland's hands, as a victory for Norway over Brazil on the final matchday would ensure their progression, thus eliminating both Scotland and Morocco regardless of their result. But few expected such a victory for Norway, and the mood in Scotland's camp remained broadly optimistic, despite a general sense that performances in the first two matches had merited more than a solitary point.

On Thursday 18 June it was back onto the superb St

Rémy training pitch, which was never a chore in the brilliant French sunshine. In *The Game of My Life*, Craig Brown describes keen anticipation among the squad during this period, and in *A Bhoy's Own Story*, Paul Lambert describes a harmonious and hardworking camp, with players enjoying each other's company between training sessions. Pool competitions with prize money kept players occupied in-between watching the World Cup and going for walks in St Rémy to pass the time. On occasional evenings, the squad also went out for a meal together in St Rémy, with Lambert later describing a particularly poor restaurant choice by charismatic masseur Stewart MacMillan which led to the squad threatening to throw MacMillan into the hotel swimming pool!

On Friday 19 June, the delegation were invited to attend a reception organised by the mayor of St Rémy at the town hall. This gave the squad a second chance to wear their kilts, and it seemed the entire town turned out to listen to the mayor's speech, take photographs and collect autographs. In *The Game of My Life*, Craig Brown recollects that local schoolchildren had decorated the town hall for the occasion, and did a small concert comprising of Scottish country dancing and Scottish songs, including a rendition of 'Flower of Scotland'. After the mayor's speech, SFA President Jack McGinn then presented the town with a gift of an engraved silver plate to commemorate Scotland's stay in the town, and a buffet lunch was then laid on inside the grand building. It was almost dusk as the kilted players emerged back out onto the steps of the town hall, but hundreds of autograph hunters had nevertheless remained waiting outside for the players. John Collins of Monaco was a particular favourite of the football-mad French youngsters, and it did his status no harm that he could also comfortably converse with them in French.

With the match against Morocco scheduled for the following Tuesday, 23 June, Brown had identified Saturday 20 June as a crucial preparation day, and had correspondingly decided the players would train twice that day. Fascinatingly, Brown tells his *World Cup Diary* that his plans for these crucial sessions were somewhat derailed by goalkeeping coach Alan Hodgkinson refusing him use of the goalkeepers in the morning session, Brown stating that Hodgkinson referred to them as 'my goalies'. 'So what chance have we got of getting them?' Brown sardonically comments.

On the eve of such a crucially important match, Brown was therefore dictated to by his goalkeeping coach, and considering Brown's manner and tone when making these remarks he clearly resented his crucial Saturday sessions being undermined in this way.

On a lighter note, Craig Burley, who after his heroics against Norway was fast becoming Scotland's headline star of France 98, decided to dye his hair blond at a local hairdressing salon in St Rémy. Paul Lambert recalls that this idea had been touted by several players over a few drinks at one of the squad meal nights, but the next day Burley was the only one who followed through with it.

In *Adventures of the Golden Age*, Archie Macpherson found Burley's harmless actions interesting, and drew a distinction between the players in Craig Brown's camp and Scotland World Cup camps of the past. Macpherson states that there is no way of telling how players will react to the virtual seclusion of a major tournament camp, and in conversation with Scottish journalist Hugh Keevins, Macpherson and Keevins concurred that football players were changing in the late-1990s. Keevins is quoted in *Adventures of the Golden Age* as stating, prior to this, that Scottish journalists had been accustomed to players' behaviour getting out of hand, their being found drunk in bars or with women in their rooms. Keevins told Macpherson that he had spent time in Brown's camp during this period, and had asked Burley why he had dyed his hair, to which Burley replied, 'Ach, I just got bored, so I did it.' In Keevins' experience, this was certainly different from how players had behaved in the past when they got bored. Burley was the consummate professional in comparison, having left Cumnock, East Ayrshire, aged just 16. Having risen up through the ranks at Chelsea via a tough apprenticeship to play in the English Premier League, he was not about to throw it all away so easily.

Sunday 21 June was a ferociously hot day in the south of France. Some of the players and delegation chose to attend church in St Rémy first thing in the morning, and then only one training session was conducted in the heat, taking place at 11.30am and consisting of a full training match. Craig Brown told his *World Cup Diary* that the practice game was important for shaping up the team for the Morocco match, and that in his view things were progressing reasonably smoothly and efficiently. Brown, in his perpetual sparring match with the media, had also decided that the Sunday training session would be private. Brown later stated that this had displeased the attending media, who had grown restless on the fringes of the St Rémy training facility but had ultimately accepted his decision and kept their distance. One person who was permitted access was Wales manager Bobby Gould, father of goalkeeper Jonathan, who had come to spectate.

On return to the Valrugues Hotel in the afternoon,

Brown permitted family visitors rare access to the camp, which the players very much welcomed. Positively, Colin Calderwood had also rejoined the squad after undergoing surgery in London on his broken hand, albeit with his right arm in a sling, placing him out of contention for the next match.

In *The Game of My Life*, Craig Brown recalls missing the input of his multimedia expert from back home, Brian Hendry, in preparation for Morocco. Brown nevertheless describes having watched numerous videos of the Moroccans in advance of the tournament, as well as having travelled to Casablanca to watch them play live. In *The Game of My Life*, and in a subsequent interview given to *Open Goal*, Brown refers to Morocco as the 'reigning African champions'. However, this is a longstanding oversight on the part of Brown, as Egypt were in fact African champions at that time, having triumphed in Burkina Faso in February 1998. Morocco had in fact performed disappointingly at the tournament, exiting at the quarter-final stage to South Africa.

At France 98, Morocco were managed by Frenchman Henri Michel, who had won 58 caps for France as a player and was a 'one-club man' for Nantes, with whom he had won three French League titles. Interestingly, in 1998 Michel was also the last man to have managed France at the World Cup finals, having led them to a respectable third-place finish at Mexico 86. Michel also had history with Scotland, having lost his job as manager of France during the next World Cup qualification campaign for Italia 90, where Scotland emerged from the qualification group with Yugoslavia ahead of France, who did not qualify. A draw against Cyprus away in October 1988 had been Michel's undoing and had led to him being replaced by Michel Platini, who could not turn the tide in time. Andy Roxburgh and Craig Brown, if you recall, with their aggregate marginal gains approach, had only narrowly avoided the same fate at the hands of the Cypriots.

In terms of personnel, Morocco were certainly not to be underestimated, and in Noureddine Naybet, Mustapha Hadji and Salaheddine Bassir had three players who played for Deportivo La Coruña in the Spanish top flight. As many will recall, Deportivo of this era were one of the best teams in Europe, and indeed eventually won the La Liga title in the 1999–2000 season, with Naybet still a mainstay at the heart of their defence. Youssef Chippo (Porto), Abdelilah Saber (Sporting Lisbon), Abdelkrim El Hadrioui (Benfica), and Taher El Khalej (Benfica) were also vastly experienced internationals plying their trade in the Portuguese top flight.

In *The Game of My Life*, Craig Brown also highlights that Morocco are a nation with seven times the population of Scotland, and who were also higher than Scotland in the FIFA world rankings in 1998. Morocco were undoubtedly another football-obsessed country, with their interest having exploded in 1986 after they topped a World Cup qualification group ahead of European heavyweights England, Portugal and Poland to become the first African nation to qualify for the last 16 of the World Cup. No wonder that Morocco's insatiable appetite for football has led to the nation bidding to host the World Cup finals on no fewer than five occasions at time of writing (1994, 1998, 2006, 2010, and 2026): their five failed hosting bids are also a record number of failures, which one hopes might one day be rectified.

Early on Monday 22 June, the Scottish delegation prepared for their third and final journey of the France 98 first-round group stage. The match against Morocco the following day would be held in Saint-Etienne, where Scotland had faced off against France in their November 1997 friendly match. Prior to leaving the Valrugues Hotel, veteran goalkeeper Jim Leighton provided the *World Cup Diary* with an insight into his long-held pre-match superstitions. Leighton allowed camera access to his hotel room and showed off his blue under-jersey that had been with him everywhere since his early career at Aberdeen. As Leighton held aloft the tattered garment, it barely displayed a washed-out number four on the back, which Leighton explained had been reprinted three times. Leighton added that, even after his departure from Aberdeen to Manchester United, Aberdeen kit man Teddy Scott sent him a number four to maintain the superstition. Leighton, a true gentleman of Scottish football, referred to this type of pre-match moment as his hardest at a World Cup, with nothing else to occupy his thoughts.

The players drifted out to their waiting coach in the usual shades and travelling attire, and the card schools got immediately underway. Then, following a short flight from Nîmes to Saint-Etienne, a waiting coach took the squad directly to the Stade Geoffroy-Guichard for their pitch training session. On arrival at the stadium, vocal members of the Tartan Army were waiting to greet the players with songs, and the players acknowledged the travelling fans.

On the *Official Scotland Podcast*, Scotland fan Martin Riddell recounts his memories of Saint-Etienne, and the general mood and thinking among the Tartan Army in the city, which was '1978 all over again' – essentially, 'Who are

Morocco?' instead of 'Who are Peru?' Riddell says fans were saying, 'It's aye, Morocco, we'll hammer Morocco' and 'Where are we going in the next game? Once we beat Morocco, where is the next game? It was going to be in Marseille, I think.' Fans were already figuring out how to get by train from Saint-Etienne down to Marseille for the next match.

For the squad, following their training session, there was one night's stay at the Mercure Hotel in Saint-Etienne. On the *World Cup Diary*, John Collins addresses the camera in French, saying, '*Nous allons gagner!*' – 'We are going to win!'

On Tuesday 23 June, both Scotland versus Morocco and Brazil versus Norway were scheduled to kick off at 9pm local time. Consequently, this was Scotland's longest wait for kick-off so far on a matchday, and the players had mostly chosen to rest in their hotel rooms to conserve their energy. Craig Brown, as usual, took the time to address his *World Cup Diary*, informing the camera that the mood in the camp remained very positive. Brown described a calm assurance among the players, and being absolutely convinced he would get the best effort from the players chosen to start.

On the *Official Scotland Podcast*, Kevin Gallacher discusses Scotland's mentality on the eve of the Morocco match. 'I think we looked at the Moroccans as being very weak. Probably weaker than Estonia,' Gallacher comments. 'I think, personally, we went out and underestimated them.'

When the moment finally arrived, the squad boarded their coach from the hotel, looking confident in their navy suits and royal blue shirts. Craig Burley in particular, with his new peroxide-blond hairstyle, caught the eye of the *World Cup Diary*, as he joked confidently before boarding the coach. On arrival at the Stade Geoffroy-Guichard, the Tartan Army had as usual taken over the city in their thousands, and the nearby pubs were decked out in a sea of flags and tartan. Perpetual choruses of 'Flower of Scotland' were heard loudly around every corner, and soon those fortunate enough to have a match ticket would descend upon the 36,000-capacity stadium, expectant of Scotland's first win of the tournament.

Craig Brown had made two straightforward changes from Scotland's 1–1 draw with Norway, with David Weir replacing the injured Colin Calderwood, and Jackie McNamara in for the suspended Darren Jackson. These changes meant Scotland would start the match as they had finished against Norway, with Burley switched into his preferred central midfield position. Having displayed such a strong finish against Norway, this team was no surprise, with both Weir and McNamara having made a significant impact after coming off the bench against the Norwegians in Bordeaux.

In order of squad numbers, the Scotland team named to face Morocco on 23 June 1998 were in 3–5–2 formation as follows: Jim Leighton (1); Jackie McNamara (2); Tom Boyd (3); Colin Hendry (5); Kevin Gallacher (7); Craig Burley (8); Gordon Durie (9); John Collins (11); Paul Lambert (14); David Weir (16); Christian Dailly (22).

In order of squad numbers, the Morocco team lined up as follows in a 4–5–1 formation: Abdelilah Saber (2); Smahi Triki (5); Noureddine Naybet (6); Mustapha Hadji (7); Abdeljalil Hadda (9); Driss Benzekri (goalkeeper) (12); Salaheddine Bassir (14); Lahcen Abrami (15); Gharib Amzine (17); Youssef Chippo (18); Tahar El Khalej (20).

The two teams emerged at the same time to the usual capacity crowd and electric atmosphere, by now customary for a Scotland match at France 98. Scotland were back in their navy Umbro home shirt, white shorts and red socks, with opposition Morocco wearing white shirts with red trim, green shorts and white socks. The match officials wore striking yellow shirts and black shorts, led by referee for the evening, Ali Mohamed Bujsaim of the United Arab Emirates. At the conclusion of the national anthems, Colin Hendry shook hands with Moroccan captain Noureddine Naybet, and after the coin toss, Scotland's final group match had arrived.

First Half

Morocco kicked off, and their playing style immediately looked different from anything Scotland had faced in qualification, preparatory friendlies or the tournament itself. This was the first time that Scotland and Morocco had faced each other in an international football match, and from the opening exchanges Scotland visibly struggled to come to terms with Morocco's style of play.

There is little doubt that Craig Brown's Scotland had by now proved themselves more or less the equal of most European opponents. And Brazil, with so many of their top stars playing for European clubs, had also been fairly 'European' in their playing style in the opening match. This type of encounter had suited Scotland, their rock-solid defence, clever and economical midfield and hard-running forward line proving awkward opposition for some of the best the world had to offer at the time. Morocco, on the other hand, played football on the other end of the spectrum, and Scotland looked unsettled from the first passages of play.

For starters, Morocco had a tendency to chip the ball around, with looping passes somehow always more or less reaching their intended destination. Scotland struggled with this passing style, as Hendry's aerial dominance at the back was rarely a factor with the ball cannoning around in midfield. Furthermore, Scotland's technical players such as Paul Lambert and John Collins looked bemused by the continual ricochets, which were impossible to read. Perhaps most significantly, Morocco were also quicker than Scotland to the ball, with Mustapha Hadji in particular absolutely electric when running the Moroccan right channel with the ball at his feet. Another unusual feature of the Moroccan play was their consistently accurate slide tackling, which seemed to rob Scotland's midfielders time and again as they tried to get a hold of the ball and dictate the play. These factors combined to force Scotland into trying to play Morocco at their own game, but this was never going to work with such a pace differential and with Scotland looking so uncomfortable.

Another factor was the referee who, in my view, was the weakest to officiate a Scotland match at France 98. Time and again, he appeared to ignore the Moroccan centre-back Smahi Triki clattering through the back of Gordon Durie and Kevin Gallacher, which consequently negated Scotland's usually successful hold-up play. Moroccan goalkeeper Driss Benzekri, identified as a potential weakness and almost dropped before the match, also continually rode his luck by rushing off his line to clear Scotland's advances with a range of unorthodox punches and wild swipes at the ball. Overall, Scotland had unwittingly walked into a perfect storm, and increasingly they did not have the answers to the questions being posed by the Moroccans as the first half wore on.

On 22 minutes, the inevitable happened. Morocco won a free kick in their right-back position after high feet from Christian Dailly. Triki played the kick short to captain Naybet, who returned the ball to Benzekri, who fed left-back Lahcen Abrami, who then found rangy Benfica midfielder Tahar El Khalej. In a split second, in a moment that encapsulated the malaise that had engulfed Scotland in the first 20 minutes, El Khalej fired an awkward looping pass right through the heart of the Scottish defence. Such was the trajectory of the pass, Hendry could not meet the ball in the air in his usual style, and the lightning-quick Salaheddine Bassir took off and darted between Hendry and Tom Boyd, easily reaching the ball first. Bassir, in behind Scotland's back line in acres of room, then unleashed a terrific left-footed strike from a tight angle. The ferocious shot beat Jim Leighton at his near post, a cardinal sin for a goalkeeper, but in fairness this was a shot that could have beaten any goalkeeper on any given day. More concerningly for Scotland, it was a goal that had looked likely for several minutes before it came.

The diminutive Bassir reeled away in jubilation, arms outstretched and looking to the sky. Perhaps the quickest player on the pitch, none of his team-mates could catch him initially as they tried to mob him in celebration. Leighton looked absolutely disgusted as he picked the ball out of the net. However, the Tartan Army had not given up just yet, and a powerful chorus of 'Flower of Scotland' rose up within the Stade Geoffroy-Guichard.

In his *World Cup Diary*, Craig Brown states that, in his view, the first 20 minutes of the match were very even, but the more cynical might have asked which match Brown was watching. Even so, on a night which looked doomed to failure all too quickly, Scotland were denied a stonewall penalty only moments after the Moroccans took the lead. A Scotland goal kick had reached Dailly, on the halfway line, who then fed Craig Burley after Morocco halted his own efforts to break forwards. With a superb pass, Burley then fed clubmate Jackie McNamara, who had raced down the right wing. McNamara fired a dangerous cross into the Moroccan penalty area that left-back Abrami blocked with his hand. Referee Bujsaim waved play on, dismissing the vigorous Scottish appeals and denying Scotland a clear penalty for the second match in a row. Out of all the first-half passages of play, this was perhaps the moment that snuffed out any realistic hope Scotland might have had of reversing the tide against their African opponents.

Thereafter, Scotland rallied before half time, with the erratic Benzekri easily able to turn an innocuous cross into a goalmouth scramble, but somehow it just never looked like Scotland might capitalise on the frequent loose balls that bounced around inside the Moroccan penalty area. Indeed, more often than not, the loose ball would be fed to Hadji to launch yet another blistering counter-attack, with Scotland's defenders caught forward. Morocco deployed this tactic so often in the first half that it can only have been deliberate on the part of the wily Henri Michel, who was looking as cool as a cucumber in the Moroccan dugout in his beige suit.

Half Time

The *World Cup Diary* captures a silent Scotland dressing at half time in Saint-Etienne. The players, all seated, take fluids on board as Brown stands in the centre of the dressing room and tells his players to remain calm and 'get the self-belief back' and that they have to realise Scotland are the better side. Specifically, Brown instructs them to use the left channel, where Jackie McNamara had always been 'in oceans of space'. Finally, he reminds them that they have '45 minutes, do or die.' As usual, Brown's right-hand man Alex Miller interjects at the perfect moment without interrupting, ending the team talk positively. 'The longer the game goes, do not panic,' Miller reminds the players. 'Because a draw could take you through if Brazil win it [versus Norway]. It's all square there. So let's be calm, cool and collected, OK? We know we can do better.'

Second Half

Craig Brown's men perhaps knew they could do better, but disastrously, and for the second match in a row, Scotland then lost a goal in the first minute of the second half. A Scottish move broke down deep inside Moroccan territory, resulting in Smahi Triki chipping yet another early looping pass over Scotland's defence. This time, David Weir was wrong-footed, and Morocco's main striker Abdeljalil Hadda was able to run in behind the struggling defender. Hadda outstripped Weir for pace, and controlled the ball superbly with his head, before hitting an unusual early chipped shot directly at the onrushing Jim Leighton. In complete shock, Leighton tried to adjust his body shape to deal with the peculiar strike, but could only palm the ball directly up into the air. The shot, however, had incredible backspin, and in slow motion curved into the net, with Leighton flailing wildly in an unsuccessful effort to claw the ball to safety.

In his autobiography, *In the Firing Line*, Leighton describes the loss of this goal as 'quite simply, an avoidable and embarrassing blunder'. On the other hand, one of Leighton's main strengths was his awareness, anticipation and speed off his line. For the second time just in this tournament, Tom Boyd's own goal against Brazil being the other occasion, Leighton had been extremely unlucky when deploying a goalkeeping method that had saved Scotland on countless other occasions. In truth, in a career spanning over 600 appearances in the top flights of Scotland and England, and over 91 international caps, Leighton would rarely have faced such an unorthodox team, who were quite simply impossible to predict on the night.

Eight minutes later, Brown's men and the passionate Tartan Army knew their World Cup dream was almost definitely over. Following another passage of play that included yet another crazy punch on the ball by Moroccan goalkeeper Driss Benzekri, Craig Burley had shown good skill to drift past Mustapha Hadji and shove the ball inside to Paul Lambert, who knocked to ball into the path of Colin Hendry, whose ambitious shot on goal did not reach Benzekri and which Morocco headed clear. Salaheddine Bassir, a constant thorn in Scotland's side, dropped into his own half and controlled the loose ball superbly on his chest, before arcing his run to create yet another counterattack opportunity. With Hendry caught out of position, Burley then scythed down Bassir from the back in a moment of madness. It was the classic 'tackle from behind' that FIFA had sought to outlaw at the tournament, with the drama increased by Bassir's histrionics as he rolled across the turf, feigning agony. In a typically uncertain display of refereeing, Ali Mohamed Bujsaim initially produced a yellow card from his pocket but appeared to be influenced by the Moroccan players, who mobbed him and pointed to Bassir's faux agony. Inevitably, befitting one of the Scotland National

Team's worst ever evenings, Bujsaim then switched his yellow card for his red, which he then raised aloft in a swift motion, as if to convince the world he had had the measure of the situation all along. The blond-haired Burley, for whom the evening had promised so much, stood hands-on-hips initially, before turning and walking towards the tunnel. The replay showed, at best, that Burley had perhaps mistimed a typical midfield tackle to break up play. However, there was a definite element of recklessness and frustration in his movement that was always likely to spell trouble for him.

In *Adventures in the Golden Age*, Colin Hendry is quoted expressing disappointment that his team-mate committed such a tackle when Scotland were two goals down. Hendry describes Burley as a great player, who provided a main goal threat, and that his sending off left the team crippled for the rest of the match. Between 54 minutes, when Burley was sent off, and 85 minutes, when Bassir added a third for Morocco with a shot which deflected off Hendry, the Tartan Army rarely would have witnessed a Scotland side so thoroughly out of a football match.

On the *Official Scotland Podcast*, Kevin Gallacher offers his view of the disaster that unfolded in Saint-Etienne, which was that Morocco had 'played us off the park' and were 'so energetic'. Scotland, certain they could fashion a result and qualify if Brazil defeated Norway, underestimated Morocco, who, in Gallacher's view, 'wanted it, probably that little bit more than what we did'. Gallacher describes the 'horrible feeling' immediately after the loss. 'It was really weird,' he adds. 'I know we had to go round and see the fans, but we just wanted the ground to lift up and just swallow us up.'

In *Adventures in the Golden Age*, Colin Hendry is quoted

echoing Gallacher's sentiments. Hendry states that in his view Scotland did indeed underestimate Morocco in Saint-Etienne, and concedes he had never played against a team from Africa in his whole career until that match. Hendry adds that Scotland did not turn up as a team on the night, and were bickering and arguing on the pitch about their positioning, which was highly unusual for the group.

The sole opposing voice who does not concede Morocco were the better team on the night belongs to our main protagonist, Craig Brown. Indeed, even in his most recent interviews, such as the one given to *Open Goal* in 2019, Craig Brown maintains that, statistically, Scotland were the better team on the night, taking exception to Archie Macpherson's analysis in *Adventures of the Golden Age*, which called the evening 'embarrassing'.

Full Time

As the anguished Scotland team sat dejectedly in their dressing room after the match, their heartbreak on the night was secondary to the devastation felt by Morocco. Unbelievably, Norway had come from one goal behind to score two goals in the last seven minutes of their match against Brazil in Marseille, thus eliminating Morocco despite their own heroic 3–0 victory in Saint-Etienne.

As the news filtered onto the pitch, the Moroccans' ecstasy turned to agony, as head coach Henri Michel carried the details of their first-round exit to his crestfallen players. Scotland, perennial masters of glorious failure, had now been outdone by their African counterparts as the first round's biggest hard-luck story. Had Scotland won so convincingly on the night, one can only imagine the agony of learning of Norway's incredible and unlikely late comeback against the world champions, which provided pragmatist Egil Olsen with the last laugh in Group A. In this moment, Morocco undoubtedly became the 'African Scotland'.

But whatever the maths in Group A, the Tartan Army's dream of Scotland playing in the World Cup's knockout stages once again came to an end in 'the Cauldron' on that evening in Saint-Etienne. Brazil had finished on six points, Norway on five, Morocco on four and Scotland on just one point. The round of 16 now beckoned, but for Craig Brown's valiant heroes, it was time to say *au revoir*.

12

AFTER THE CARNIVAL

France 98 was over for Scotland, but the story was not quite finished for Craig Brown who, following Scotland's elimination, was asked by the BBC to join the Radio 5 Live commentary team. Brown gratefully accepted the invitation, and in *The Game of My Life* reflects he was privileged thereafter to travel the length and breadth of France, covering many superb matches as the tournament progressed.

France 98 still had a long way to run, with Group A not the only section to have produced final matchday drama. As in Chapter Seven, which acted as a reference guide, this chapter tells the dramatic story in brief of how the rest of France 98 panned out for the legendary, the lucky and the plucky who had survived the group stages.

First Round

Group B:
    Italy – 7 points

Chile – 3 points
Austria – 2 points
Cameroon – 2 points

Italy faced off against Austria in Saint-Denis on the final matchday, with Chile facing Cameroon in Nantes. Italy were in pole position in the group with four points from a possible six, after a 2–2 draw with Chile and 3–0 victory over Cameroon in matches one and two. Italian striker Christian Vieri, with three goals in his first two matches, was an early contender for the tournament's Golden Boot, and the return of Roberto Baggio to Italy's starting line-up, ahead of Alessandro Del Piero, was unexpected. Chile's Marcelo Salas had lived up to the pre-tournament hype, also netting three goals in his first two matches.

It took a late goal from Roberto Baggio to edge Italy over the line as group-winners with a 2–1 win over Austria. The big talking point, however, arose in the other match. With Chile unexpectedly labouring against Cameroon, and the match tied at 1–1, Cameroon's François Omam-Biyik, scorer of the famous goal that had embarrassed Argentina at Italia 90, appeared to score an excellent winner against another South American team. Unfortunately for Cameroon, László Vágner, Scotland's referee against Norway, mysteriously chalked off the goal, seemingly for a foul by Patrick Mboma in the build-up, which appeared unbelievably harsh. The furious reaction from the Cameroon bench provided some of the first round's lasting images.

Group C:
France – 9 points

Denmark – 4 points
South Africa – 2 points
Saudi Arabia – 1 point

Despite the pre-tournament worries of the French press and public, Aimé Jacquet's France were impressive in their first three matches, completing the first round as one of only two teams with a perfect record. Monaco's duo of 20-year-olds, Thierry Henry and David Trezeguet, delivered four goals between them (three for Henry and one for Trezeguet), with Christophe Dugarry, Youri Djorkaeff, Emmanuel Petit and Bixente Lizarazu also pitching in with goals. Indeed, France's total of nine first-round goals was two higher than any other nation, rubbishing pre-tournament fears that they were a team who could not score.

The major downside for France during the first round was a red card for their talisman Zinedine Zidane, whose fragile temperament had broken against Saudi Arabia on matchday two. With France 2–0 up and cruising, Zidane had inexplicably raked Saudi defender Mohammed Al-Khilaiwi with his studs, leading to a two-match suspension for 'Zizou'. Denmark, inspired by the Laudrup brothers, Brian and Michael, and despite a stuttering draw against South Africa, were deserved second-place qualifiers.

Group D:
Nigeria – 6 points
Paraguay – 5 points
Spain – 4 points
Bulgaria – 1 point

Group D was an enthralling affair, characterised by the mesmerising performances of group-winners Nigeria, and the self-fulfilling prophecy of Spain coach Javier Clemente, who had been convinced that Spain had been drawn in the most difficult group. Nigeria appeared able to score goals from anywhere, and Spain never really recovered from their 3–2 loss to Nigeria in their opening match. France 98 had appeared one tournament too many for veteran Spanish goalkeeper Andoni Zubizarreta, whose abysmal goalkeeping error led to Spain's capitulation against Nigeria from a winning position. Then, with only a draw against Paraguay in their second match, Spain were on the ropes.

Spain's knockout blow came on the final matchday. With Nigeria already group-winners with a game to spare, Spain had to hope that the Nigerians remained motivated against the resilient Paraguay, who after two draws were still very much in the hunt. In the end, Spain held up their end of the bargain, smashing the hapless Bulgarians 6–1, but Paraguay had too much for the cruising Nigerians, defeating them 3–1, with their second from Miguel Angel Benítez one of the goals of the tournament. Spain's exit was undoubtedly the biggest shock of the first round.

Group E:
   The Netherlands – 5 points
   Mexico – 5 points
   Belgium – 3 points
   South Korea – 1 point

Group E was another tight affair, the outcome of which was not decided until the final minutes of the last matchday.

The Netherlands and Belgium, such familiar adversaries, had begun with a 0–0 draw in Saint-Denis, and Mexico had got off to a good start with a 3–1 victory over South Korea. Mexico's two-goal hero on the day had been blond-haired striker Luis Hernández, another who appeared to be living up to the pre-tournament hype. The Netherlands, with a crushing 5–0 win over South Korea on matchday two, announced themselves as one of the tournament's teams to watch, while Belgium could only manage a 2–2 draw with Mexico.

Therefore, it was all to play for on the final matchday, but with the Netherlands 2–0 up against Mexico and Belgium winning against South Korea, Group E appeared to be reaching an expected conclusion. However, everything changed with just 20 minutes remaining. After a host of missed Belgian chances, South Korea stole an unlikely equaliser, and Mexico rallied, scoring with 15 minutes remaining and again in the final minute through Hernández to earn a 2–2 draw against the Netherlands. Mexico were through and Belgium were out.

Group F:
   Germany – 7 points
   Yugoslavia – 7 points
   Iran – 3 points
   USA – 0 points

Group F had played out true to form and, going into the final matchday, Germany and Yugoslavia only had to hold their nerve against Iran and the USA to qualify, which they duly did, 2–0 and 1–0 respectively.

The group's crucial match, Germany versus Yugoslavia, had ended in a 2–2 draw in Lens, but had required a typical late rally from Germany for the match to end even. With Yugoslavia 2–0 up and cruising, a lucky own goal with 15 minutes remaining provided the Germans with a lifeline, and Oliver Bierhoff scored an inevitable late header to equalise for Germany.

In the group's other big story, Iran had defeated the USA 2–1 in Lyon, in the much-discussed political grudge match. Ultimately, the match itself was played out with the utmost respect, with pre-match photographs taken and gifts exchanged in an effort to demonstrate peace through football.

Group G:
  Romania – 7 points
  England – 6 points
  Colombia – 3 points
  Tunisia – 1 point

With England and Romania beating Tunisia and Colombia respectively on the opening matchday, England versus Romania in Toulouse on matchday two always looked likely to decide first and second place in Group G. After some controversial team selections, and with England trailing 1–0 to the Romanians, England manager Glenn Hoddle finally let 18-year-old wonderkid Michael Owen off the leash. Owen rewarded Hoddle with a goal six minutes later, but then England inexplicably allowed Chelsea's Dan Petrescu (previously signed by Hoddle for Chelsea in 1995 and whom Hoddle would later sign again for Southampton in 2000 after his return to English club management) in behind to score a last-minute winner.

With Romania safely through, England versus Colombia on the final matchday was a straight shootout for the second qualification place in Group G. The match, however, was all but over as a contest by the 30-minute mark, following a superb goal from Darren Anderton and then a fantastic curling free kick from David Beckham, to give England a 2–0 victory in Lens.

Group H:
- Argentina – 9 points
- Croatia – 6 points
- Jamaica – 3 points
- Japan – 0 points

Argentina were the second team to emerge from the first round with a perfect record. With four goals from three matches, including a hat-trick against Jamaica, powerful striker Gabriel Batistuta was the early frontrunner for the tournament's Golden Boot award. The performances of attacking midfielder Ariel Ortega had also lit up the first round. Argentina, with seven goals scored and zero conceded, had the look of strong tournament contenders.

Of Group H's three tournament debutants, the free-flowing and technical Croatia were the strongest by a considerable margin and, in Real Madrid's Davor Šuker, they had a player who could hit the back of the net. Robert Prosinečki, with his goal against Jamaica, became the first-ever player to score for two countries at the World Cup finals, after previously netting for Yugoslavia at Italia 90.

Second Round

Italy 1–0 Norway
27 June, Marseille

Egil Olsen's number was up in Marseille as Cesare Maldini's Italy finally disposed of the stubborn Norwegians and their direct football. Arguably the worst team in Group A, Norway had somehow found a way to finish second, but their methods had won them few friends along the way. A Christian Vieri goal in the 18th minute won this forgettable match. A long searching pass from the Italian defence split the Norwegian defence, leaving the clinical Vieri free to dispatch a low drive past Frode Grodås in the Norwegian goal.

Brazil 4–1 Chile
27 June, Paris

In the second round, Brazil performed close to their full potential in Paris against their South American counterparts, with the match over as a contest before half time thanks to two goals in the first 27 minutes from an unlikely source in César Sampaio. With Ronaldo winning and converting a penalty just before the break, Brazil gave themselves an insurmountable 3–0 half-time lead, with the talented Chile having folded under the weight of the occasion. Marcelo Salas did pull one back for Chile on the 68th minute, his fourth of the tournament, but Ronaldo promptly killed off the Chileans two minutes later with his second of the match, a cool finish following an assist from Denílson.

France 1–0 Paraguay
28 June, Lens

Hosts France went marching on after a historic extra-time winner from goalscoring centre-back Laurent Blanc. After a nervy 0–0 draw in normal time, Blanc's terrific strike, scored in the 113th minute after Robert Pires and David Trezeguet had combined, was the first golden goal ever scored at the World Cup. France, although deserved winners, had missed the creativity of suspended playmaker Zinedine Zidane on the day.

Nigeria 1–4 Denmark
28 June, Saint-Denis

In perhaps the surprise of the second round, Denmark hammered four past the best of the Africans, Nigeria, in the Stade de France. Not for the first time in the tournament, the Danes got off to a quick start, and were two goals to the good after just 12 minutes. Also competent in defence, Denmark thereafter rarely offered Nigeria any realistic route back into the match, and killed the game off in the second half with two more goals, with Laudrup brothers Brian and Michael having a field day by this point. The flamboyant Nigerians were able to pull back a late consolation goal, but it was the unfancied Danes who were now catching the eye.

Germany 2–1 Mexico
29 June, Montpellier

France 98 had so far been far from a vintage World Cup for Germany. Having trailed to Yugoslavia in the group stages, Germany also found themselves 1–0 down to Mexico with only 15 minutes remaining in Montpellier. Again, Luis Hernández had been Mexico's goalscoring hero with his fourth of the tournament. Germany, however, so predictably by now, refused to be beaten, and reversed the deficit in a typically epic comeback, hitting Mexico twice in nine minutes through captain Jürgen Klinsmann and Oliver Bierhoff. With two goals each from the group stages, Klinsmann and Bierhoff had now snuck up to three tournament goals each in total. Given their incredible World Cup record, few were writing off Germany at this stage.

The Netherlands 2–1 Yugoslavia
29 June, Toulouse

Many now considered the Netherlands the best football team at the tournament, but Yugoslavia also had an abundance of talent, and provided stiff second-round opposition for the Dutch. Dennis Bergkamp, perhaps at the peak of his powers at France 98, had given the Netherlands a deserved half-time lead, but Yugoslavia rallied and drew level just after half-time through Slobodan Komljenović. With Yugoslavia in the ascendancy, the pivotal moment of the match came when Jaap Stam was penalised for pulling the jersey of Vladimir Jugović in the box. Unfortunately for Yugoslavia, Predrag Mijatović smashed the resulting penalty against the crossbar to let the Netherlands off the hook. In the last minute of the match, Edgar Davids then gained redemption following his Euro 96 nightmare, by grabbing the winner with a superb long-range strike.

Romania 0–1 Croatia
30 June, Bordeaux

This second-round exit for Romania spelled the end of a golden era for Romanian football, with successful coach Anghel Iordănescu set to step down after the tournament and veteran talisman Gheorghe Hagi retiring from international football. Croatia, fast becoming the surprise package of the tournament, had marginally too much for the Romanians, and the match was settled by a penalty from Davor Šuker. The referee ordered a penalty retake for Croatian encroachment after Šuker scored with his initial effort, but Šuker showed nerves of steel, dispatching the retaken spot-kick past Bogdan Stelea as well.

Argentina 2–2 England AET
(Argentina won 4–3 on penalties)
30 June, Saint-Etienne

In perhaps the match of the second round, England were 2–1 up after just 16 minutes, following converted penalties by Gabriel Batistuta and Alan Shearer, and a solo wondergoal by FIFA Young Player of the Tournament, Michael Owen. England looked to be heading in at the break with a lead, but were hit with a sucker punch right on half time, after a superbly worked free kick resulted in an equaliser from Javier Zanetti. With no more goals in the match, the other major incident was the 47th-minute dismissal of David Beckham, shown the red card for a petulant flick out at Diego Simeone right in front of the referee.

In the only second-round match decided by penalties, England bowed out, following misses from Paul Ince and David Batty from the spot. England's major tournament Achilles heel had struck again.

Quarter-finals

Italy 0–0 France AET
(France won 4–3 on penalties)
3 July, Saint-Denis

In a match dominated by so many players who knew each other from Italy's Serie A, and with so much at stake, it did not come as any great surprise that Italy versus France ended in a goalless stalemate. Even with their playmaker Zinedine Zidane back from suspension, France lacked the cutting edge to break down the ultra-defensive Italians. The match was all about the drama of the penalty shootout, and when Bixente Lizarazu missed first for France, the host nation held their breath and feared the worst. It was Italy, however, who had lost the 1994 World Cup Final on penalties, who came unstuck once again in a penalty shootout. To France's relief, balance was first restored following a miss from Demetrio Albertini, and Laurent Blanc then piled on the pressure with the decisive fourth kick for France. The unfortunate Luigi Di Biagio then hit the crossbar for Italy, and with his save from Albertini, Fabien Barthez in the French goal was the national hero on the day. With this book being Scotland's France 98 story, it should also be acknowledged that Scottish official Hugh Dallas refereed this match, a highly commendable achievement.

Brazil 3–2 Denmark
3 July, Nantes

In what proved to be a superb encounter, surprise package Denmark ran the holders and favourites close. Having once again got off to a flying start with a goal inside two minutes from Martin Jørgensen, Denmark had Brazil rattled. The *Seleção* had nevertheless proved themselves resilient as well as technical in previous matches, and pulled level just nine minutes later through Bebeto. Brazil then took the lead before the break with a superb clipped shot by Rivaldo, but the Danes refused to go down without a fight, drawing level five minutes after the restart through Brian Laudrup after an error from Roberto Carlos. In the end, though, it was a day that belonged to Brazilian number ten Rivaldo, who struck the winner with a superb left-footed, low-driven shot from 25 yards, which beat Peter Schmeichel at his left-hand post. For Danish captain Michael Laudrup, so influential in Denmark's superb run to the quarter-finals, it was the end of an international career spanning over 100 caps.

The Netherlands 2–1 Argentina
4 July, Marseille

In a tournament of redemptions for the Netherlands, Patrick Kluivert was next in line. Kluivert had not started since being sent off in the Netherlands' first group-stage match against Belgium, but with a goal in the 12th minute of the quarter-final, the 21-year-old striker maintained his reputation for scoring goals that really mattered. Five minutes later, however, the Netherlands shipped their lead cheaply, when a poorly played offside trap allowed Claudio

López to race clear and beat Edwin van der Sar with a cheeky nutmeg. In a match that seemed destined for extra-time, Argentina had gone closest to finding the winner, hitting the woodwork twice, through Gabriel Batistuta and Ariel Ortega. There was also the dramatic interlude of Arthur Numan's red card for two bookable offences, and Ortega's straight red card for a nonsensical headbutt on van der Sar. Then, with extra time looming large, Frank de Boer hoisted a long searching ball forwards towards Dennis Bergkamp. Like all great players, Bergkamp was occasionally capable of seeing passages of play one or two steps ahead of everyone else on the field, and cushioned de Boer's pass with his right foot, before stunning the ball once again with his right to wrong-foot Argentinian defender Roberto Ayala. Having now made the half-yard he required in the penalty box, Bergkamp then curved a shot with the outside of his right foot into the top left-hand corner of Argentina's net. With three deft touches, Bergkamp had scored one of the goals of the tournament, and the Netherlands were in the semi-finals.

Germany 0–3 Croatia
4 July, Lyon

After a relatively even first period, the last quarter-final tipped towards Croatia within the space of five eventful minutes just before the half-time interval. Following a crude foul on Davor Šuker, German defender Christian Wörns received a straight red card that left the Germans reeling, and then five minutes later Robert Jarni struck a powerful low shot past Andreas Köpke to leave Germany with a mountain to climb. Of course, overcoming difficult odds at the World Cup was fairly normal for Germany, but they left themselves with far too much to do on this occasion, and two further late goals from Goran Vlaović and Šuker provided the 1998 World Cup with its first major shock. This was Šuker's fourth goal of the competition so far, placing himself tied in second place in the race for the tournament's Golden Boot.

Semi-finals

Brazil 1–1 The Netherlands AET
(Brazil won 4–2 on penalties)
7 July, Marseille

For many, this match constituted the 'final before the final', with the Netherlands and Brazil arguably the best two teams of the tournament so far. After a disappointing first half, the match sprang to life in the first minute of the second half, when Rivaldo picked out Ronaldo with a superb left-footed pass. Following a perfect left-footed first touch, Ronaldo was suddenly in behind the Dutch defence and, with incredible strength and speed, held off the lunging Phillip Cocu, before sweeping the ball past Edwin van der Sar with his left foot. Ronaldo, a truly two-footed player, was almost impossible to defend against in these types of situations in his prime, and Brazil had a 1–0 lead.

Brazil's lead held for almost the entire second half, until the 87th minute, when Ronald de Boer somehow found acres of space on the Dutch right, and swung a superb cross into the Brazilian penalty box. Patrick Kluivert, who had been guilty of missing chances earlier in the match, rose highest and bulleted a perfect header into the Brazilian net.

In a World Cup semi-final graced by goals from two truly special young talents, 21-year-old Kluivert had now cancelled out 21-year-old Ronaldo's opener. However, neither team found a winning goal, and the match went to penalties.

Going into the shootout, many thought van der Sar might have the edge over Taffarel, and that the Dutch penalty-takers would maintain their composure compared to the Brazilians. In reality, the opposite was true, as Brazil netted all four of their penalties in emphatic fashion, and did not require a fifth after misses from Cocu and Ronald de Boer. Taffarel had dominated the shootout with two heroic saves, and goalkeepers, normally much maligned in Brazil, now had their place in Brazilian World Cup history. The *Seleção* had reached the World Cup Final.

France 2–1 Croatia
8 July, Saint-Denis

Similarly to the first semi-final, after a relatively even first 45 minutes, France versus Croatia sprang to life in the first few minutes of the second half. However, the opening goal did not fall the way of the hosts, as anticipated, and it was the predatory Davor Šuker who found space in behind the French defence to break the deadlock with a cool left-footed shot past Fabien Barthez. The frenetic start to the second period did not end there, as Croatia's lead lasted only a minute. Right-back Lilian Thuram came from nowhere to link with Youri Djorkaeff and dispatch the ball past goalkeeper Dražen Ladić. Twenty-two minutes later, Thuram then wrote his name into French football folklore after bustling forwards on the right once more, linking with Thierry Henry and firing an unstoppable left-footed shot into the bottom left-hand corner of the Croatian net. France would hold on to win a place in their first World Cup Final, but not before centre-back Laurent Blanc was sent-off for lashing out at Croatian defender Slaven Bilić. A suspension for the World Cup Final was rough justice for Blanc, who had played superbly throughout the tournament, and Bilić won few friends for the theatrical manner in which he had reacted. Blanc's crushing loss was defender Frank Leboeuf's gain, as he would now replace Blanc in France's starting line-up for the World Cup Final.

Third-place play-off

The Netherlands 1–2 Croatia
11 July, Paris

As shock semi-finalists, the 1998 third-place play-off match always seemed to favour Croatia, with the Netherlands seemingly unable to fully motivate themselves after being fancied by so many to go all the way. After Robert Prosinečki's opener on 13 minutes, Boudewijn Zenden equalised for the Netherlands just eight minutes later with one of the goals of the tournament, a ferocious strike that left Dražen Ladić helpless. Inevitably, it was Davor Šuker who settled the match with a 36th-minute strike, his sixth goal of tournament, one more than Christian Vieri and Gabriel Batistuta, to win the tournament's Golden Boot. Croatia's third-place finish at their first World Cup finals was a truly spectacular achievement, with people no longer laughing at head coach Miroslav Blažević's optimistic pre-tournament predictions.

Final

Brazil 0–3 France
12 July, Saint-Denis

The 1998 World Cup Final will always be as much remembered for what occurred off the pitch, pre-match, as for what occurred on it. On the day of the final, Brazilian star Ronaldo allegedly experienced a seizure of an unconfirmed nature at Brazil's hotel headquarters. Ronaldo was subsequently taken to hospital in Paris, leaving his team-mates rattled, and Edmundo had replaced Ronaldo in Brazil's starting eleven on the original teamsheets distributed at the Stade de France. What happened to Ronaldo, and why he was then suddenly passed fit to play in the World Cup Final at the very last moment, has been the subject of theories and speculation for over two decades. Some speculate that the CBF's contract with Nike had a specific clause relating to Ronaldo, stating he must play if passed fit to do so. Therefore, if true, and following his discharge from hospital in Paris, Ronaldo was contractually compelled to start the match, regardless of his apparent health issues on the day. Either way, the team sheets were reissued, and Ronaldo played, a shadow of the player he could be.

With Ronaldo out of sorts, and Brazil clearly affected by the day's drama, France, and one man in particular, dominated the final itself. Zinedine Zidane's moment had arrived, and with two superb first-half headers from corners, 'Zizou' ruthlessly exposed Brazil's lethargy. With a brace in a World Cup Final on home soil, in 45 minutes Zidane had become a national icon, and the triumphant French added a third from Emmanuel Petit in the last minute of the match to put the result beyond doubt. France, so dominant on the day, could even afford to play the last 20 minutes with ten men, after Marcel Desailly was sent off for a second bookable offence. Nothing, however, was going to halt *Les Bleus* in their march towards their first World Cup win, and when little midfield general Didier Deschamps lifted the famous trophy above his head, few grudged this talented team their place at football's summit.

AFTERWORD
THE REVOLVING DOOR

So, there you have it, as in 1954, 1958, 1974, 1978, 1982, 1986 and 1990, Scotland's World Cup story of 1998 concluded with a first-round exit. Craig Brown, like all his predecessors, had failed to deliver the holy grail of reaching the second round at a major tournament with Scotland. Even so, Scotland's France 98 journey had swept the nation along, and for one glorious afternoon in the Stade de France, the eyes of the entire world had watched Scotland play football, and play it well. On 10 June 1998, Colin Hendry, John Collins, Paul Lambert, Craig Burley and company had proved that they could compete with the best, and, had they not been Scotland, would most likely not have conceded a bizarre own goal with 17 minutes remaining.

Overall, one cannot help but wonder what the outcome might have been had Scotland hung on for a well-earned draw against Brazil, and then beaten Norway, which they undoubtedly deserved to do. Alas, it was not to be, and in the end, France 98 was Scotland's eight World Cup tournaments in microcosm, providing the history books with yet another Scottish capitulation against unlikely opponents, as if to restore balance to the football universe. It seems only Scotland could come so far, achieve so much, play so well when it mattered, and yet still experience a first-round exit with just one solitary point.

Football is a fickle sport, but unlike in more recent times where the sack is the least the fans or media expect after failure, the SFA did not dispense with Craig Brown's services after the Morocco match, and nor did he feel he should resign honourably. Instead, Brown and Scotland focused on Euro 2000 qualification. Again, typically for the Scotland National Team, this was about fine margins, a touch of bad luck and, ultimately, disappointment. Drawn in Group 9 with Euro 96 finalists the Czech Republic, surprising absentees from France 98, Scotland performed well enough across their 10 matches with five wins, three draws and only two defeats. But they were no match for the Czechs, who destroyed the rest of the group with 10 wins from 10 games. Scotland faced a play-off against – who else? – the Auld Enemy.

Again, hard luck was a factor. Paul Lambert had been injured playing for Celtic in the Old Firm derby on 7 November 1999, just six days before the play-off first leg against England at Hampden Park, colliding face-first with Rangers' Jorg Albertz in his own penalty box. To add insult, literally, to injury, Lambert had conceded a penalty and Albertz had scored from the spot while Lambert was being stretchered off and heading for dental surgery. Rangers won the pulsating match 4–2, but Brown was already looking wistfully at plans for the following Saturday, as Lambert was 'the most consistent performer in the country', as Brown said at the time. In the match on 13 November, England won 2–0 with a brace from Paul Scholes, and Brown later suggested that Lambert would have marked Scholes, had he played, and the result at Hampden might have been different. There was still the matter of the second leg, and despite many fans and commentators seeing the match on English soil as a foregone conclusion, Scotland upset the odds with a 1–0 victory at Wembley on 17 November 1999 from a 39th-minute Don Hutchison goal.

But it was still a narrow 2–1 aggregate defeat for the Scots and, after the match, England defender Tony Adams told Brown that England had been lucky to progress to the Euro 2000 tournament in Scotland's place. Brown also said later that English people would often mention that Scotland performance in London with admiration – surely cold comfort. Once again, after such valiant efforts, a single goal had robbed the Scotland National Team of a tournament.

In World Cup 2002 qualifying, between September 2000 and October 2001, Scotland battled valiantly in UEFA Group 6, a tough group containing both Belgium and Croatia, and again it came down to fine margins. Things had begun well with a last-minute Neil McCann goal in Latvia sealing all three points in the first match, and Scotland did finish the group with a creditable four wins, three draws and a single defeat. But Scotland's fate rested on a last-minute goal for Belgium in the fixture at Hampden Park on 24 March 2001. The Scots were 2–0 up thanks to a Billy Dodds double, the second from a penalty after Belgian defender Eric Deflandre had handled on his own goal line and been sent off. Somehow, 10-man Belgium clawed their way back into the game, and this time it was Daniel Van Buyten who struck late to break Scotland hearts and make the final score 2–2. Scotland's only defeat was subsequently to Belgium, in Brussels in September 2001, and they would eventually finish in third place on 15 points, pipped by the Belgians on 17. But for Van Buyten, Scotland would have progressed to the play-offs in second place behind Croatia with 17 points to Belgium's 16, and we would be telling another story.

On 6 October 2001, Scotland beat Latvia 2–1 at Hampden Park in the final qualifier, but Croatia also beat Belgium by a single goal to snuff out Scotland's unlikely chances of overhauling either of them. After the Latvia match, at the post-match press conference, an emotional Craig Brown resigned as Scotland manager, stating that he had personally made the decision some time previously that this would be his last campaign, and that he had told the players after they left the Hampden pitch, which had also been 'emotional'. Brown was clear that 'there was no pressure' from the SFA to resign, and that, after 15 years with the Scotland set-up, leaving would be 'a wrench'.

Brown would go on to have moderate success in English football in his latter career at Preston North End and Derby County, before returning to Scotland for spells as manager of Motherwell and Aberdeen, then deciding to retire in 2013 at the age of 72.

But what of Scotland in those intervening years after Brown's exit and the present day? The story of the Scotland National Team and the revolving door through which Scotland managers frequently came and went in the 2000s and 2010s is enough for another book in itself, but this statistic is clear: between 1986 and 2001, Scotland were managed by two men, Andy Roxburgh and Craig Brown, across 132 matches. Between 2001 and 2021, 10 managers have taken the helm across the next 170 games – Berti Vogts, Tommy Burns (as caretaker), Walter Smith, Alex McLeish, George Burley, Craig Levein, Billy Stark (caretaker), Gordon Strachan, Malky Mackay (caretaker), Alex McLeish (for a second spell) and finally Steve Clarke. Until Clarke's appointment, Scotland failed to qualify for another major tournament, as

Brown's sides had done. Some managers were sacked, while others could not resist the lure of managerial vacancies in club management.

Only when Clarke was appointed in 2019 did Scotland's fortunes – and luck – finally change. After a win against Cyprus in Clarke's first competitive match, Scotland suffered several defeats that ruled out automatic qualification for Euro 2020. But, on 12 November 2020, they won a dramatic penalty shoot-out 5–4 to deny Serbia in the new UEFA Nations League and take their place in the coronavirus-delayed pan-continental Euro 2020 tournament. It was all a long time coming!

Despite his protestations about the crushing defeat by Morocco in 1998, Brown had undoubtedly done a tremendous job since his appointment as Scotland manager in 1993, first in building a resilient team, and thereafter in steering them to two consecutive major tournaments. The exemplary professionalism shown by his squad at France 98 was a testament to Brown's leadership, and he evidently believed in his team so much that, well over two decades later, he continued to defend their poorest performance under his stewardship. In many hundreds of pages and many hours of spoken interviews since France 98, Brown has never once publicly criticised any of his France 98 group, and despite the passing of the years, has still at times appeared to consider himself their manager and protector. Brown has indeed defended his France 98 group to the last, and is this also not the mark of a great manager? In terms of the history of the Scotland National Team, this is certainly a category in which Craig Brown belongs.

ABOUT THE AUTHOR

Neil Doherty is a graduate of Glasgow Caledonian University, where he obtained a Bachelor of Arts degree with first-class honours. Neil embraces the highs and lows of being a season ticket holder with Kilmarnock FC and member of the Scotland National Team Supporters Club. Neil has a professional career unrelated to football, and his spare-time passion for football research and writing has now given rise to his first book, *World Cup 1998: Scotland's Story*.

www.neildoherty.org.uk

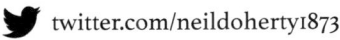 twitter.com/neildoherty1873

ACKNOWLEDGEMENTS

This book is dedicated to my dad Martin. Thanks Dad, for the early experiences of Hampden terrace culture, for countless trips to Rugby Park, and for the more recent memories from the Nou Camp, Old Trafford, Westfalen, Stade de France and others. As my critique partner, your words of encouragement, suggestions and editing assistance were also crucial in the writing process.

I would also like to thank my beautiful wife Liz, for listening to my ramblings about 90s football, manuscript deadlines and the rest. Football is not a subject you care too much about, but as with everything, I could not have done it without you. I love you.

Mum, John, Karrie, Maggie and Hayley, you are all inspiring people, and I am so fortunate you are my family.

Thanks also to Eleanor, Stevie and Paul, for your encouragement and guidance.

A final thanks to editor Alex Hazle and cover designer James Pople for your skill and professionalism. Again, I feel fortunate you both believed in my writing project, and I doubt I could have found two nicer guys to work with.

REFERENCES & BIBLIOGRAPHY

BBC Sport: 'Lambert out of play-offs' (1999).

BBC Sport: 'Brown announces resignation' (2001).

Bellos, A: *Futebol* (Bloomsbury Publishing Plc, London, 2014).

Blake, H & Calvert, J: *The Ugly Game* (Simon & Schuster UK Ltd, London, 2015).

Borchert Holm, N: *The Fifa Family: A Love Story* (Amazon Prime documentary video stream, 2017).

Brassell, A: *Football Ramble Meets... Arséne Wenger* (Farnborough, Stakhanov Industries Ltd podcast, 2020).

Brewin, J: 'One team in Tallinn: when Scotland kicked off against nobody – and still didn't win' (FourFourTwo.com, 2014).

Brown, C & Bale, B: *Craig Brown: The Autobiography* (Virgin Books, London, 1998).

Brown, C: *The Game of My Life* (Blake Publishing Ltd, London, 2003).

Flanagan, C: 'Ole Gunnar Solksjær – "I got to Old Trafford and a guy thought I was on a tour"' FourFourTwo.com, 2016).

Goodlad, P: 'Scotland: Craig Brown regrets leaving out Ally McCoist from 1998 World Cup squad' (BBC Sport, 2018).

Goram, A & King, I: *The Goalie* (Mainstream Publishing Ltd, Edinburgh, 2009).

Hamilton, G: *The World Soccer Essential Guide: France 98 (Parts 1–4)* (Publisher Sean Singleton, London, 1998).

Henson, M: 'José Mourinho, Fabio Capello, André Villas-Boas: How Largs shaped them' (BBC Sport, 2019).

Lambert, P & Clark, G: *A Bhoy's Own Story* (Mainstream Publishing Ltd, Edinburgh, 1998).

Leighton, J & Robertson, K: *In the Firing Line* (Mainstream Publishing Ltd, Edinburgh, 2000).

Macpherson, A: *Adventures in the Golden Age* (Black & White Publishing Ltd, Edinburgh, 2018).

McCall, S & Nixon, A: *The Real McCall* (Mainstream Publishing Ltd, Edinburgh, 1998).

McDougall, M: 'Paul Lambert reveals details behind infamous Celtic "smell the glove" taunt as he dismisses Andy Goram rumours' (DailyRecord.co.uk, 2020).

Moore, N: 'Craig Burley on France 98: you may as well play Brazil, score a goal, dye your hair, and get sent off' (FourFourTwo.com, 2014).

Newby, S & Zanelli, T: *Well done Michael he's 13, episode 8: Darren Young* (podcast, 2020).

Open Goal: 'Si Ferry meets... Craig Brown' (Open-Goal.co.uk, 2019).

Perez, J-L: *Planet FIFA* (Amazon Prime documentary video stream, 2016).

Radnedge, K & Hamilton, G: 'Group A – Group H', *World Soccer*, Vol 38, no 10, p32–97 (1998).

Radnedge, K & Hamilton, G: 'The Final – Squads', *World Soccer*, Vol 38, no 11, p4–67 (1998).

Scotsport Extra Time: *Scotland fans in Bordeaux France 98* (YouTube, 2020).

Shepherd, R: 'Saint or sinner?' *The Express on Sunday definitive World Cup guide*, June 7, p4 (1998).

The Scottish Football Association: *Scotland vs Estonia: match programme* (Inglis Allen, Kirkcaldy, 1997).

The Scottish Football Association: *Craig Brown's World Cup Diary* (United Kingdom, Green Umbrella/Proactive Sports Management, 2001).

The Scottish Football Association: *André Villas-Boas at the Scottish FA Pro Licence 2018* (YouTube, 2018).

The Scottish Football Association: *The Official Scotland Podcast: The 1998 World Cup Revisited* (Glasgow, 2021).

Third, P: 'How Craig Brown set up Scotland to tackle Brazil's Ronaldo at France 98' (The Press and Journal online, 2020).

Wilson, J: *Inverting the Pyramid: The History of Football Tactics* (Orion Books Ltd, London, 2008).

Yallop, D: *How They Stole the Game* (Constable & Robinson Ltd, London, 2011).

Printed in Great Britain
by Amazon